The Pocket Guide to

Critical Thinking

Second Edition

Richard L. Epstein

Advanced Reasoning Forum

WADSWORTH

™

THOMSON LEARNING

Australia • Canada • Mexico • Singapore
Spain • United Kingdom • United States

Philosophy Editor: *Steve Wainwright*
Assistant Editor: *Kara Kindstrom*
Editorial Assistant: *Anna Lustig*
Marketing Manager: *Worth Hawes*
Marketing Assistant: *Justine Ferguson*
Copy Editor: *Carolyn Kernberger*
Illustrations: *Alex Raffi*
Print buyer: *Robert King*
Printer: *Webcom*

Research for this project was supported
by the *Advanced Reasoning Forum*.

Printed in Canada.
    3 4 5 6 7 06 05 04 03

0-534-56102-0

For more information about our
products,
contact us at:
**Thomson Learning Academic
Resource Center
1-800-423-0563**

For permission to use material from
this text,
contact us by:
**Phone: 1-800-730-2214
Fax: 1-800-731-2215
Web: www.thomsonrights.com**

Asia
Thomson Learning
60 Albert Complex, #15-01
Albert Complex
Singapore 189969

Australia
Nelson Thomson Learning
102 Dodds Street
South Street
South Melbourne, Victoria 3205
Australia

Canada
Nelson Thomson Learning
1120 Birchmount Road
Toronto, Ontario M1K 5G4
Canada

Europe/Middle East/South Africa
Thomson Learning
Berkshire House
168-173 High Holborn
London WC1 V7AA
United Kingdom

Latin America
Thomson Learning
Seneca, 53
Colonia Polanco
11560 Mexico D.F.
Mexico

Spain
Paraninfo Thomson Learning
Calle/Magallanes, 25
28015 Madrid, Spain

The Pocket Guide to Critical Thinking
Second Edition

Preface

This little book is meant as a summary and guide to the art of reasoning well in daily life.

Critical thinking is evaluating whether we should be convinced that some claim is true or some argument is good, as well as formulating good arguments. Critical thinking is something we need to do every day.

I've summarized here the most important ideas about the subject. But critical thinking is more than knowing definitions and rules and a few examples. It requires judgment. The full story, with lots of examples and exercises is in my textbook *Critical Thinking*. Use this *Pocket Guide* as a place to start learning how to reason well and write good arguments, or as a summary for reference. Your practice can come from using these ideas every day watching television, reading the newspaper, talking to your friends, working at your job.

In this second edition sections have also been added on reasoning in the sciences: observations vs. deductions, experiments, models, and explanations.

The short chapters here can be read more or less independently, though a familiarity with the material in Chapters 1–7 is assumed in all the following chapters.

Because your reasoning can be sharpened, you can understand more, you can avoid being duped. You can reason well with those you love and work with and need to convince. But whether you will do so depends not just on method, not just on the tools of reasoning, but on your goals, your ends. And that depends on virtue.

1 Claims

Reasoning well begins with being able
to recognize and make both claims
and definitions.

> **Claim** A declarative sentence used in such a
> way that it is either true or false (but not both).

Dogs are mammals. *Claim.*

$2 + 2 = 5$ *Claim.*

Dick is hungry. *Claim.*

How can anyone be so dumb as to think that cats can reason?
Not a claim. Questions aren't claims.

I wish I could get a job.
Claim or not claim depending on use. If Maria, who's been trying
to get a job for three weeks says this to herself, it's not a claim: It's
more like a prayer or an extended sigh. But if Dick's parents are
berating him for not getting a job, he might say, "It's not that I'm
not trying. I wish I could get a job." He could be lying, so in this
context "I wish I could get a job" would be a claim.

> **Vague Sentence** A sentence used in such a
> way that it is unclear what the speaker intended.

If we can't understand what someone is saying, we can't
say it's true or false. But everything we say is somewhat
vague. After all, no two people have identical perceptions,

1

and since the way we understand words depends on our experience, we all understand words a little differently.

You say, "My English professor showed up late for class on Tuesday." Which Tuesday? Who's your English professor? What do you mean by late? 5 minutes? 30 seconds? How do you determine when she showed up? When she walked through the door? At exactly what point? When her nose crossed the threshold? That's silly. We all know "what you meant."

The issue isn't whether a sentence is vague, but whether it's too vague, given the context, for us to be justified in saying it has a truth-value.

Too vague
You can win a lot playing blackjack.
Our dish soap is new and improved.
People who are disabled are just as good as people who aren't.

Drawing the line fallacy It's a mistake to argue that if you can't make the difference precise, there is no difference.

Example If a suspect who is totally uncooperative is hit once by a policeman, then that's not unnecessary force. Nor twice, if he's resisting. Possibly three times. If he's still resisting, shouldn't the policeman have the right to hit him again? It would be dangerous not to allow that. So, you can't tell me exactly how many times a policeman has to hit a suspect before it's unnecessary force. So the policeman did not use unnecessary force. This convinced the jury in the first trial of the policemen who beat up Rodney King. But it's a bad argument. We may not be able to draw a precise line that always discriminates between unnecessary and necessary force, but we can distinguish extreme cases.

The Supreme Court of Montana on vague laws:

A statute is void on its face if it fails to give a person of ordinary intelligence fair notice that his contemplated conduct is forbidden. . . .

It is a basic principle of due process that an enactment is void for vagueness if its prohibitions are not clearly defined. Vague laws offend several important values. First, because we assume that man is free to steer between lawful and unlawful conduct, we insist that laws give the person of ordinary intelligence a reasonable opportunity to know what is prohibited, so that he may act accordingly. Vague laws may trap the innocent by not providing fair warning. Second, if arbitrary and discriminatory enforcement is to be prevented, laws must provide explicit standards for those who apply them. A vague law impermissibly delegates basic policy matters to policemen, judges, and juries for resolution on an ad hoc and subjective basis, with the attendant dangers of arbitrary and discriminatory application.

Subjective Claim   A claim is *subjective* if whether it is true or false depends on what someone (or something) thinks, believes, or feels. A subjective claim invokes **personal standards**.

A claim that is not subjective is **objective**. Objective claims use **impersonal standards**.

Suppose Harry says:

"New cars today are really expensive."

If Harry means that new cars cost too much for him to feel comfortable buying one, then the claim is subjective. If Harry has in mind that the average cost of a new car is more than twice the federal government poverty standard for a family of four, then he would be using impersonal standards, and it is objective. Or Harry may have no standard in mind, in which case it's too vague to be a claim.

If it is not clear what standard is being invoked, don't argue about the claim. The sentence is too vague.

All ravens are black. *Objective*

My dog is hungry. *Subjective.*

It's cold outside.
Subjective claim. Too vague to be an objective claim.

Wanda weighs 215 lbs.   *Objective.*

Wanda is fat.   *Subjective.*

Abortion is wrong.
Not a claim. Too vague, unless it's made clear what standard is being used.

I'm feeling romantic tonight.
Too vague. This isn't even clear enough to be a subjective claim.

Confusing objective and subjective   It's a mistake to treat a subjective claim as objective, or vice versa.

Thinking a subjective claim is objective
— That tie is hideous. I'm not going to a party with you like that.
— What are you talking about? This tie is great. It's the style.
— You're crazy. It's ugly.

Thinking an objective claim is subjective
— (Student) I deserve a higher mark in this course.
— (Teacher) No you don't.
— (Student) That's just your opinion.

> **Ambiguous Sentence**   A sentence such that there are two, or only a very few, clear ways to understand it.

An ambiguous sentence is not a claim until we decide which way to understand it.

Ambiguous
Zoe saw the waiter with the glasses.
Dr. E's dogs eat over 10 pounds of meat every week.
    (Ambiguous between the group and the individual:
    Each dog or all the dogs together eat that much?)

> **Definition**   An explanation or stipulation of how to use a word or phrase.

 Definitions are not claims. A definition is not true or
false, but good or bad, apt or wrong. A *persuasive*
definition is a claim masquerading as a definition.
For example: "Abortion is the murder of unborn children."
What should be debated is being assumed in the definition.
Beware of and do not use persuasive definitions.

"Dog" means "domestic canine". *Definition.*

Puce is the color of a flea, purple brown or brownish purple.
Definition.

A dog is a man's best friend.
Not a definition. Not a claim, either, because it's too vague.

A feminist is someone who thinks that women are better
than men.
Persuasive definition.

— Maria's so rich, she can afford to buy you dinner.
— What do you mean by "rich"?
— She's got a Mercedes.
Not a definition (or a very bad one). Some people who have a
Mercedes aren't rich, and some people who are rich don't own one.
That Maria has a Mercedes is some *evidence* that she's rich.

The type A person is one who exhibits the following behavioral
characteristics: constant hurriedness, free-floating hostility, and
intense competitiveness.
Bad definition. The words doing the defining are too vague.

Fasting and very low calorie diets (diets below 500 calories) cause
a loss of nitrogen and potassium in the body, a loss which is
believed to trigger a mechanism in the body that causes us to hold
on to our fat stores and to turn to muscle protein for energy instead.
 Jane Fonda's New Workout and Weight Loss Program
Definition. Definitions are not always labeled, but are often made
in passing. This is a good definition of "very low calorie diet."

> ***Good Definition***   A good definition satisfies both:
> - The words doing the defining are clear and better understood than the word or phrase being defined.
> - The words being defined and the defining phrase can be used interchangeably. That is, it's correct to use the one exactly when it's correct to use the other.

Often getting a good definition and showing that it works is a major piece of research.

Species are groups of interbreeding natural populations that are reproductively isolated from each other.

E. Mayr, Populations, Species and Evolution.

Analysis Consider two kinds of crows in Europe: the black crow and the hooded crow. The former is completely black, while the latter is part black and part grey. These used to be called different species, but some intermediate forms occur due to interbreeding in various places; biologists now classify those kinds as subspecies. It seems that they take the word "isolated" in Mayr's definition to mean "total isolation"; by that definition species can't interbreed.

Other biologists point to species that are highly isolated but do interbreed, just in very restricted areas and only rarely. They are interpreting Mayr's definition in terms of relative isolation. For them, species can interbreed. The "deep" question about whether species can interbreed turns into a question about how to *define* "species."

Steps in making a good definition
1. Show the need for a definition.
2. State the definition.
3. Make sure the words make sense.
4. Give examples where the definition applies.
5. Give examples where the definition does not apply.
6. If necessary, contrast it with other likely definitions.
7. Possibly revise your definition.

2 Concealed Claims

> Someone tries to convince us by a choice of words rather than an argument—the subtleties of rhetoric in place of good reasoning.

Slanter Any literary device that attempts to convince by using words that conceal a dubious claim.

Slanters are bad because they try to get us to assume a dubious claim is true without reflecting on it. Here are some kinds of slanters.

Loaded Question A question that conceals a dubious claim that should be argued for rather than assumed.

When are you planning to start studying in this course?
Why don't you love me anymore?
Why can't you dress like a gentleman?

The best response to a loaded question is to point out the concealed claim and begin discussing that.

Euphemism (yoo'-fuh-mizm) A word or phrase that makes something sound better than a neutral description.
Dysphemism (dis'-fuh-mizm) A word or phrase that makes something sound worse than a neutral description.

"Freedom fighter"—the guerillas are good people fighting to liberate their country and give their countrymen freedom.

"Terrorist"—the guerillas are bad people, inflicting violence on civilians for their own partisan ends without popular support.

> ***Downplayer*** A word or phrase that minimizes the significance of a claim.
>
> ***Up-player*** A word or phrase that exaggerates the significance of a claim.

Zoe: Hey Mom. Great news. I managed to pass my first French exam.

Mom: You only just passed?

Zoe has up-played the significance of what she did, concealing the claim "It took great effort to pass" with the word "managed." Her mother downplayed the significance of passing by using "only just," concealing the claim "Passing and not getting a good grade is not commendable."

One way to downplay is with words that restrict or limit the meaning of others, what we call *qualifiers*—like my promise that if you buy this book you will pass this course.*

A *weaseler* is a claim that's qualified so much that the apparent meaning is no longer there.

Dick (to his boss): I am truly sorry that it has taken so long for you to understand what I have been saying.

> ***Proof Substitute*** A word or phrase that suggests the speaker has a proof, but no proof is actually offered.

Dr. E: By now you must have been convinced what a great teacher I am. It's obvious to anyone. Of course, some people are a little slow. But surely you see it.

Dr. E didn't prove that he is a great teacher, though he made it

---

* Purchaser agrees to study this book four hours per day during the term.

sound as if he were proving something. He was just reiterating the claim, trying to browbeat you into believing it with the words "obvious," "some people are slow," "surely," "must have been convinced."

Another way to conceal that you have no support for your claim is to *shift the burden of proof*.

— You should vote for Senator Ruiz.
— Why?
— Why not?

Any concealed claim is an *innuendo*. But usually we use that term for concealed claims that are really unpleasant.

— Where are you from?
— New York.
— Oh, I'm sorry.

You may be tempted to use slanters in your own writing. Don't. Slanters turn off those you want to convince. Worse, though they may work for the moment, they don't stick. Without reinforcement, the other person will remember only the joke or jibe. A good argument can last and last—the other person can see the point clearly and reconstruct it. And if you use slanters, the other person can destroy your points not by facing your real argument, but by pointing out the slanters.

> If you reason calmly and rationally you
> will earn the respect of the other, and may
> learn that the other merits your respect, too.

3 Arguments

The point of an argument is to convince that a claim—the conclusion—is true. The conclusion is sometimes called the *issue* that is being debated.

Argument   An *argument* is a collection of claims, one of which is called the **conclusion** whose truth the argument is intended to establish; the others are called the **premises**, which are supposed to lead to, or support, or convince that the conclusion is true.

Critical thinking is the most important subject in school. It will help you reason better, and it will help you get a job, and it will help you do better in all your other classes.

Premises: Critical thinking will help you reason better. Critical thinking will help you get a job. Critical thinking will help you do better in all your other classes.
Conclusion: Critical thinking is the most important subject in school.

Sheep are the dumbest animals. If the one in front walks off a cliff, all the rest will follow. And if they get rolled on their backs, they can't right themselves.

Premises: If the sheep in front walks off a cliff, all the rest will follow. If sheep get rolled on their backs, they can't right themselves.
Conclusion: Sheep are the dumbest animals.

Out? Out? I was safe by a mile. Are you blind? He didn't even touch me with his glove!
Premise: He didn't even touch me with his glove.
Conclusion: I was safe.

Follow the directions for using this medicine provided by your doctor. This medicine may be taken on an empty stomach or with food. Store this medicine at room temperature, away from heat and light.
Not an argument. Instructions or commands are not an attempt to convince anyone that some claim is true.

How come you don't call me? What's wrong? You don't love your mother? Where did I go wrong?
Not an argument. Not every attempt to persuade is an attempt to convince that a claim is true.

> ***Indicator Word*** A word or phrase added to a claim to tell us the role of the claim in an argument or what the speaker thinks of the claim or argument.

Conclusion indicators: hence; therefore; so; thus; consequently; we can then show that; it follows that; . . .

Premise indicators: since; because; for; in as much as; given that; suppose that; it follows from; on account of; due to; . . .

Indicators of speaker's belief: probably; certainly; most likely; I think; . . .

A claim is ***dubious*** or ***implausible*** if we have no good reason to believe that it is true, yet are not sure it's false. If we know that a claim is true or have very good reason to believe it is true, we say the claim is ***plausible***.

> ***Good Argument*** An argument in which the premises give good reason to believe the conclusion is true.

For an argument to be good, it must pass two tests:

• There should be good reason to believe the premises.

• The premises lead to, support, establish the conclusion.

In Chapter 4 we'll see criteria for what counts as good reason to believe a premise. In Chapter 5 we'll spell out what we mean for a conclusion to follow from the premises. Here we can note that the two tests are independent of each other:

Premises support the conclusion,
but one of the premises is false.
You are reading this book.
Everyone who reads this book is a man.
So you are a man.

Premises and conclusion true,
but premises don't support the conclusion.
You are reading this book.
This book was printed in the U.S.
Therefore, this book costs less than $30.

If one of the premises of an argument is dubious, then we have no reason to accept the conclusion. From a false premise we can derive both true claims and false claims. ***An argument is no better than its least plausible premise.***

False premise, true conclusion.
Lassie is a cat.
All cats have fur.
So Lassie has fur.

False premise, false conclusion.
Lassie is a dog.
All dogs can fly.
So Lassie can fly.

4 Evaluating Premises

We can establish criteria for when we should accept the premises of an argument.

Three Attitudes We Can Take to the Truth of a Claim
- Accept the claim as true.
- Reject the claim as false.
- Suspend judgment.

---

not believe ≠ believe is false
lack of evidence ≠ evidence it is false

1. *Our most reliable source of information about the world is our own experience.*

But claims based on our own experience are no better than our memory and the functioning of our senses at the time of the experience. We reject or don't accept a claim about our own experience if either:

- We have good reason to doubt our memory.
- The claim contradicts other experiences of ours, and there is a good argument (theory) against the claim.

The world is flat.
Reject our experience. There is a good theory against the claim.

My date was gone from the room for over an hour at the party.
Suspend judgment? If you were drunk, don't accept this.

A claim might seem to be about your own experience, yet is really a conclusion drawn from your experience.

If you meet two Chinese students who are good at math, you're justified in claiming "Two Chinese students are good at math," not "All Chinese students are good at math."

2. We can accept claims that are made by someone we know and trust and who is an authority about that kind of claim.

Zoe tells Harry to stay away from the area of town around S. 3rd. She's seen people doing drugs there and knows two people who have been held up in that neighborhood. Zoe is reliable, and her knowledge would matter about these claims.

Tom's mother tells him that he should major in business so he can get ahead in life. Should he believe her? She can tell him about her friends' children. But what are the chances of getting a good job with a degree in business? It would be better to check at the local colleges where they keep records on hiring graduates. He shouldn't reject her claim; he should suspend judgment until he gets more information.

3. We can accept claims that are made by a reputable authority whom we can trust as an expert on this kind of claim and who has no motive to mislead.

The Surgeon General announces that smoking is bad for your health. He's got no axe to grind. He's a physician. He's in a position to survey the research on the subject. Believe him.

But the doctor hired by the tobacco company says there's no proof that smoking is addictive or causes lung cancer. Is he an expert on smoking-related diseases? Or perhaps an allergist or pediatrician? It matters for whether to trust his ability to interpret the data. And he has a motive to mislead. There's no reason to accept his claim.

The new Surgeon General says that marijuana should be legal. What kind of authority is she on this subject? Is she a politician? A lawyer? What kind of expertise does she have on matters of law and public policy? She is an authority figure, but not an expert on *this* kind of claim. No reason to accept it.

4. We can accept a claim put forward in a reputable journal or reference source.

The New England Journal of Medicine is regularly quoted in newspapers, and for good reason. The articles in it are subjected to peer review: Experts in the subject are asked to evaluate whether the research was done to scientific standards.

The National Geographic has less reliable standards, since they pay for their own research in order to sell their magazine. But it's pretty reliable about natural history and ethnography.

What about the *Dictionary of Biography*? There's probably no motive for bias in it, though it may be incomplete. Yet it's often hard to get a better source of information about, say, a 19th century physician.

On the other hand, anyone can incorporate as "The Advanced Reasoning Forum," or any other title you like. A name is not enough to go by.

5. *We can accept a claim from a media source that is usually reliable and has no obvious motive to mislead.*

With newspapers, television, radio, magazines, and other media sources it's partly like trusting your friend and partly like trusting an authority. The more you read a particular newspaper, the better you'll be able to judge whether to trust its news gathering as reliable. The more you read a particular magazine, the better you'll be able to judge whether there's an editorial bias.

Some factors you can use to evaluate a news report:
• The source has been reliable in the past.
• The source doesn't have a bias on the topic.
• The source being quoted is named.

There's never good reason to accept a claim from an unnamed source.

A television network consistently gives a bias against a particular presidential candidate. So when it says that the candidate contradicted himself twice yesterday, you should take it with a grain of salt. That may be true, but it may be a matter of interpretation. Or it may be plain false.

"Usually reliable sources" are not even as reliable as the person who is quoting them; anyway they've covered themselves by saying "usually."

There are no absolute rules for when to accept, when to reject, and when to suspend judgment about a claim. It's a skill, weighing up the following in order of importance:

Reject:	The claim contradicts personal experience. (Exceptions: Our memory is not good; there's a good argument against our understanding of our experience; it's not our experience at all, but what we've concluded from it.)
Accept:	The claim is known by personal experience.
Reject:	The claim contradicts other claims we know to be true.
Reject:	Two claims used as premises contradict each other.
Accept:	The claim is made by someone you know and trust and who is an authority about that kind of claim.
Accept:	The claim is offered by a reputable authority whom you can trust as an expert about this kind of claim and who has no motive to mislead.
Accept:	The claim is put forward in a reputable journal or reference source.
Accept:	The claim is in a media source that's usually reliable and has no obvious motive to mislead.

Arguing backwards   Believing the premises because the conclusion is true is bad reasoning.

All dogs bark.
Spot is a dog.
So Spot barks.

The conclusion is true, and the argument is valid. So "All dogs bark" is true? No—there are lots of dogs that don't bark (basenjis).

An argument is supposed to convince us that its conclusion is true, not that its premises are true.
Learn when to *suspend judgment*.

The following are bad arguments, common mistakes in applying the criteria, *if* the generic premise is false.

Appeal to authority   A bad argument that uses or requires as premise:

"(Almost) anything that _____ says about ____ is true."

— What do you think of the new seat belt law?
— It must be bad, 'cause William Buckley said so.

Mistaking the person for the claim   A bad argument that uses or requires as premise:

"(Almost) anything that _____ says about ____ is false."

Mistaking the person for the argument   A bad argument that uses or requires as premise:

"(Almost) any argument that _____ gives about ____ is bad."

Zoe: I went to Professor Zzzyzzx's talk about writing last night. He said that the best way to start on a novel is to make an outline of the plot.
Suzy: Are you kidding? He can't even speak English.

Appeal to common practice   A bad argument that uses or requires as premise:

"If (almost) everyone else (in this group) does it, then it's O.K. to do."

— You shouldn't stay out so late. It's dangerous, so I want you home early.
— But none of my friends have curfews and they stay out as long as they want.

Appeal to common belief   An argument that uses or requires as premise:

"If (almost) everyone else (in this group) believes it, then it's true."

Phony refutation   An argument that uses or requires as premises both:

(i) " ____ has done or said ____ , which shows that he or she does not believe the conclusion of his or her own argument" *and* (ii) "If someone does not believe the conclusion of his or her own argument, then the argument is bad."

— We should stop logging old-growth forests. There are very few of them left in the U.S. They are important watersheds and preserve wildlife. And once cut, we cannot recreate them.
— You say we should stop logging old-growth forests? Who are you kidding? You just built a log cabin on the mountain.

— We should tax cigarettes much more heavily. It will stop kids from starting to smoke.
— I can't believe you said that. Don't you smoke three packs a day?

Whether an argument is good or bad does not depend on who made it.

Remember, the above are bad ways to evaluate claims only if the generic premise is false.

You go to England and everyone else is driving on the left-hand side. It's not wrong to conclude that you should, too.

The American Medical Association says "Smoking can cause cancer." The group is composed of reliable experts, so perhaps you should accept their claim.

"I can't solve this math question. It's too hard for a high school student. But my math teacher says the answer is 3. So the answer must be 3." This is a reliable authority.

Above all, personal experience is your best guide. Don't trust others more than yourself about what you know best.

— I played doubles on my team for four years. It is definitely a more intense game than playing singles.
— Yesterday on the news Michael Chang said that doubles in tennis is much easier because there are two people covering almost the same playing area.
— I guess he must be right then.

5 Experiments

The big revolution in science in the Renaissance came when people began looking to their own experience rather than to the ancients for evidence as to how nature works.

Observational Claim   A claim that is established either by personal experience or observation in an experiment.

Evidence   Usually the observational claims that are used as premises of an argument. Sometimes the term refers to all the claims used as premises.

Here "personal experience" means reports on what we perceive through our senses—not what we deduce from those perceptions.

What do we mean by "observation in an experiment"? A physicist may say he saw an atom traverse a cloud chamber, when what he actually saw was a line made on a piece of photographic film. A biologist may say she saw the nucleus of a cell, when what she saw was an image projected through a microscope. In both cases these people are not reporting on direct personal experience, but on deductions made from that personal experience. However, those claims made by deduction from the perceptions arising from certain types of experiments are, by consensus in that area of science, deemed to be observational.

Within any one area of science there is a high level of agreement on what counts as an observational claim. But from one area of science to another that standard may vary. A physicist beginning work in biology may well question why certain claims are taken as "obvious" deductions from experience, such as the reality of what you see through a microscope. But after the general form of the inference from such direct claims about personal experience to the observational claims are made explicit once or twice, he is likely to accept such claims as undisputed evidence. If he doesn't accept such deductions, he is questioning the basis of that science.

When new techniques are introduced into a science or when a new area of science is developing there is often controversy about what counts as an observational claim. Galileo's report of moons around Jupiter was received with considerable skepticism, because telescopes were not assumed to be accurate (indeed, at that time they distorted a lot). In ethology now you can find journal articles with very different understandings of what counts as an observation claim.

One constraint we impose on reports of observations is that they should be *reproducible.* That's how we try to evade subjectivity in science. We believe that nature is uniform. What can happen once can happen again—*if* the conditions are the same. Scientists typically won't accept reports on observations that they don't think can be reproduced.

The difficulty, always, is specifying exactly what conditions are required. It is fairly easy in chemistry and physics; less so in biology; much more difficult in psychology or ethology. It is virtually impossible in history and economics. That would seem to make history and economics not sciences, then, except to the extent that we can describe very general conditions that may recur.

6   The Conclusion Follows

A conclusion follows from the premises when the argument is valid or strong.

> *Valid Argument*   An argument where it is impossible for the premises to be true and the conclusion false (at the same time).   An argument is *invalid* if it is not valid.
>
> *Strong and Weak Arguments*   Invalid arguments are classified on a scale from strong to weak. An argument is *strong* if it is very unlikely for the premises to be true and the conclusion false (at the same time). An argument is *weak* if it is likely for the premises to be true and conclusion false (at the same time).

Either an argument is valid or it isn't. There are no degrees to it. But the strength of an argument is a matter of degree.

All dogs bark.
Ralph is a dog.
Therefore, Ralph barks.

Valid. Impossible for the premises to be true and conclusion false at the same time.

All parakeets anyone I know has ever seen or heard or read about are under 2 feet tall. Therefore, the parakeets for sale at the mall are under 2 feet tall.

Strong. Surveying all the ways the premise could be true, we think that yes, a new supergrow bird food could have been formulated and the parakeets at the local mall are really 2 feet tall, we just haven't heard about it. Or a rare giant parakeet from the Amazon forest could have been discovered and brought here. Or a UFO might have abducted a parakeet by mistake, hit it with growing rays, and the bird is gigantic. So the argument is not valid. But all these ways the premise could be true and conclusion false are *so very unlikely* that we would have very good reason to believe the conclusion if the premise is true, even though the conclusion might be false.

Good teachers give fair exams. Dr. E gives fair exams. So Dr. E is a good teacher.

Weak. Dr. E might bore his students to tears and just copy good exams from the instructor's manual. Or he might get good exams from another teacher. There are lots of possibilities that are not so unlikely.

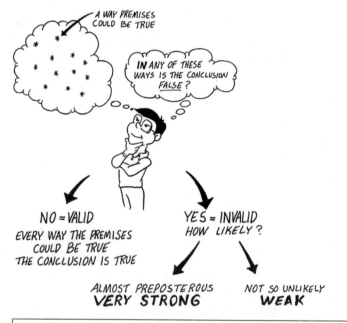

How do we show that an argument is not valid or is weak?
We give an example, a possible way in which the premises could be true and conclusion false.

To reason well you must use your imagination.

For an argument to be good, there must be good reason to believe the premises (the premises are plausible) and the conclusion must follow from the premises.

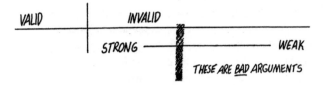

- Every good argument is valid or strong.
- Only invalid arguments are classified from strong to weak.
- Every weak argument is bad.
- Not every valid or strong argument is good
  (it could have a dubious premise).

Since an argument is intended to convince, the premises should be more plausible than the conclusion. An argument **begs the question** if its premises are no more plausible than its conclusion.

Dogs have souls.
Therefore, you should treat dogs humanely.

— God exists.
— How do you know?
— 'Cause the Bible says so.
— But why do you think that's true?
— 'Cause God wrote the Bible.

Tests for an Argument to be Good
- The premises are plausible.
- The argument is valid or strong.
- The premises are more plausible than the conclusion.

Dr. E is a philosophy professor. All philosophy professors prefer dogs to cats. So Dr. E prefers dogs to cats.
Valid, but bad. One of the premises is false.

Dick is a bachelor. So Dick was never married.
Weak, bad. Dick could be divorced.

Sandra's hair is naturally brown. Today Sandra's hair is red.
So Sandra dyed her hair.
Strong, good if the premises are true. Sandra might be taking a
new medication that has a strong effect. Or she might have been
too close to her car when they were painting it, or . . . These are
ways the premises could be true and conclusion false, so the
argument is not valid. But those ways are very unlikely, so the
argument is strong.

Prosecuting attorney: The defendant intended to kill Louise. He
bought a gun three days before he shot her. He practiced shooting
at a target that had her name written across it. He staked out her
home for two nights. He shot her twice.
Strong, good if the premises are true.

Defendant: I didn't mean to kill Louise. I only wanted to scare
her. That's what was in my mind. Only that, I swear.
Weak, bad. All he is saying may be true, yet the argument is
weak, and we have no good reason to believe the conclusion.
What he says shouldn't create reasonable doubt.

— Today's the 29th, right?
— No, it's the first.
— The first?
— Yes, yesterday was the 28th of February, and February has just
    28 days. Only in years divisible by four does it have 29 days.
Valid, good. The premises were true when this was spoken.

Whenever Spot barks, there's a cat outside. Since he's barking
now, there must be a cat outside.
Valid, but bad. Perhaps Spot is barking at the garbageman. That
doesn't show the argument is weak—it shows that the first premise
is false.

If the conclusion of a valid argument is false,
one of the premises must be false.

---

7 Repairing Arguments

Many arguments we encounter daily are not valid or strong as stated, yet they aren't really bad.

— I heard that Wanda has a pet.
— It must be a dog, because I heard barking in her house yesterday. And I know she doesn't let people bring their pets over to her home.

This is missing a premise to be a good argument: "Almost any pet that barks is a dog." But why bother saying that? Everyone knows it, and the argument is good enough without it.

In order to evaluate arguments, we need to make some assumptions about the people with whom we reason.

The mark of irrationality If you recognize that an argument is good, then it is irrational to believe the conclusion is false.

What if you hear an argument for both sides, and you can't find a flaw in either? Then you should *suspend judgment* on whether the claim is true until you can investigate more.

The Principle of Rational Discussion We assume that the other person who is discussing with us or whose arguments we are evaluating:
1. Knows about the subject under discussion.
2. Is able and willing to reason well.
3. Is not lying.

What justification do we have for invoking this principle? Not everyone fits these criteria all the time. But if someone doesn't satisfy the Principle of Rational Discussion, there's no point in reasoning with them.

- If they don't know about the subject, educate, don't debate.
- If they aren't able to reason well, teach them.
- If they aren't willing to reason well, walk away.
- If they're lying, then the only point of reasoning with them is to catch them in their lies.

Still many people don't follow the Principle of Rational Discussion. They don't care if your argument is good. Why not use bad methods of persuasion? Why should we follow these rules and assume them of others? If you don't:

- You are denying the essentials of democracy.
- You are likely to undermine your own ability to evaluate arguments.
- You are not as likely to convince others.

> If you once forfeit the confidence of your fellow citizens, you can never regain their respect and esteem. It is true that you may fool all the people some of the time; you can even fool some of the people all the time; but you can't fool all of the people all the time.
>
> Abraham Lincoln

With the Principle of Rational Discussion, we can formulate a guide to help us in evaluating arguments. Since the person is supposed to be able to reason well, we can add a premise only if it makes the argument stronger or valid and doesn't beg the question. Since the person isn't lying and knows the subject under discussion, any premise we add should be plausible, and plausible to the other person. Further, we can delete a premise if that doesn't make the argument any worse. A premise is *irrelevant* if you can delete it and the argument isn't any weaker.

> ***The Guide to Repairing Arguments***   Given an (implicit)
> argument that is apparently defective, we are justified in
> *adding* a premise or conclusion if it satisfies all three of:
>   1. The argument becomes stronger or valid.
>   2. The premise is plausible and would seem plausible
>   to the other person.
>   3. The premise is more plausible than the conclusion.
>
>   If the argument is then valid or strong, yet one of
> the original premises is false or dubious, we may *delete*
> that premise if the argument remains valid or strong.

We don't need to know what the speaker was thinking in
order to find a claim that makes the argument strong or valid,
so we take (1) to have priority over (2). By first trying to
make the argument valid or strong, we show the other person
what he or she needs to assume to make the argument good.

> ***Unrepairable Arguments***   We can't repair an
> argument if any one of the following hold:
>   • There's no argument there.
>   • The argument is so lacking in coherence
>   that there's nothing obvious to add.
>   • The premises it uses are false or very dubious
>   and cannot be deleted.
>   • The obvious premise to add would make
>   the argument weak.
>   • The obvious premise to add to make
>   the argument strong or valid is false.
>   • The conclusion is clearly false.

When you show that an argument is bad,
you haven't proved that the conclusion is false.

1. No dog meows. So Juney does not meow.

Evaluation "Juney is a dog" is the only premise that will make this a valid or strong argument. So we add that. Then, if this new claim is true, the argument is good.

 We don't add "Juney barks." That's true and may seem obvious to the person who stated the argument, but it doesn't make the argument any better. So adding it violates (1) of the Guide. We repair only as needed.

2. All dogs bark. So Ralph is a dog.

Evaluation The obvious premise to add is "Ralph barks." But then the argument is still weak (Ralph could be a seal, or a fox, or . . .). The argument is unrepairable, and hence bad.

3. Dr. E is a good teacher, because he gives fair exams.

Evaluation The unstated premise needed here is "Almost any teacher who gives fair exams is a good teacher." That gives a strong argument. But it's dubious, since a bad teacher could copy fair exams from the instructor's manual. (If you thought the claim that's needed is "Good teachers give fair exams," reread the example on p. 22.) The argument can't be repaired because the obvious premise to add to make the argument strong or valid is false or dubious.

 But can't we make it strong by adding, say, "Dr. E gives great explanations," "Dr. E is amusing," "Dr. E never misses class," . . .? Yes, all those are true, and perhaps obvious to the person. But adding those doesn't repair this argument—it makes a whole new argument.

 Don't put words in someone's mouth.

4. Tom's instructor teaches critical thinking. Tom has to pay tuition for that course. Therefore, Tom will get a passing grade in critical thinking.

Evaluation The argument is weak—and it *is* an argument: The word "therefore" tells us that. But there's no obvious way to repair it. The person apparently can't reason. It's unrepairable, and hence bad.

5. You shouldn't eat the fat on your steak. Haven't you heard that cholesterol is bad for you?

Evaluation The conclusion is the first sentence. But what are the premises? The speaker's question is rhetorical, meant to be taken as an assertion: "Cholesterol is bad for you." But that alone won't give us the conclusion. We need something like "Steak fat has a lot of cholesterol" and "You shouldn't eat anything that's bad for you." Premises like these are so obvious we don't bother to say them. This argument is O.K.

6. You're going to vote for the Green Party candidate for President? Don't you realize that means your vote will be wasted?

Evaluation Here, too, the questions are rhetorical, meant to be taken as assertions: "Don't vote for the Green Party candidate" (the conclusion) and "Your vote will be wasted" (the premise). This sounds reasonable, though something is missing. A visitor from Denmark may not know "The Green Party candidate doesn't have a chance of winning." But she may also question why that matters. We'd have to fill in the argument further: "If you vote for someone who doesn't have a chance of winning, then your vote will be wasted." And when we add that premise we see the argument that used such "obvious" premises is really not very good. Why should we believe that if you vote for someone who doesn't stand a chance of winning then your vote is wasted? If that were true, then who wins is the only important result of an election, rather than, say, making a position understood by the electorate. At best we can say that when the unstated premises are added in, we get an argument one of whose premises needs a substantial argument to convince us that it is true.

7. Cats are more likely than dogs to carry diseases harmful to humans. Cats kill songbirds and can kill people's pets. Cats disturb people at night with their screeching and clattering in garbage cans. Cats leave pawprints on cars and will sleep in unattended cars. Cats are not as pleasant as dogs and are owned only by people who have satanic affinities. So there should be a leash law for cats just as much as for dogs.

Evaluation This letter to the editor is going pretty well until the next to last sentence. That claim is a bit dubious, and the argument would be just as strong without it. So we should delete it. Then we have an argument which, with some unstated premises you can supply, is pretty good.

8. Harry's new dog is a pit bull. So it must be dangerous.

Evaluation The question here is whether we should try to make this argument valid or strong. The word "must" suggests that the speaker thinks the argument he's making is valid. Unless we have good reason to think otherwise, "must" and "have to" will signal to us that we should repair the argument as valid.

But then the only premise we could add is "All pit bulls are dangerous." And that's false. So the argument is unrepairable.

9.   In a famous speech, Martin Luther King Jr. said:

I have a dream that one day this nation will rise up and live out the true meaning of its creed: "We hold these truths to be self-evident—that all men are created equal." . . . I have a dream that one day even the state of Mississippi, a desert state sweltering with the heat of injustice and oppression, will be transformed into an oasis of freedom and justice. I have a dream that my four little children will one day live in a nation where they will not be judged by the color of their skin but by the content of their character. [Quoted from *Let the Trumpet Sound,* by Stephen B. Oates.]

. . . King is also presenting a logical argument . . . the argument might be stated as follows; "America was founded on the principle that all men are created equal. This implies that people should not be judged by skin color, which is an accident of birth, but rather by what they make of themselves ('the content of their character'). To be consistent with this principle, America should treat black people and white people alike."

The Art of Reasoning, David Kelley

Evaluation The rewriting of this passage is too much of a stretch—putting words in someone's mouth—to be appropriate. Where did David Kelley get the premise "This implies . . ."? Stating my dreams and hoping others will share them is not an argument. Martin Luther King, Jr. knew how to argue well and could do so when he wanted. We're not going to make his words more respectable by pretending they're an argument. Not every good attempt to persuade is an argument.

10. Environmentalists should not be allowed to tell us what to do. The federal government should not be allowed to tell us what to do. Therefore, we should go ahead and allow logging in old-growth forests.
Evaluation The speaker has confused whether we have the right to cut down forests with whether we should cut them down. The argument is weak; indeed, we could delete either premise and it wouldn't be any weaker. That is, the speaker's assumptions are irrelevant to the conclusion.

When someone leaves a conclusion unsaid, he is *implying* the conclusion. When you decide that an unstated claim is the conclusion, you are *inferring* that claim. We can also say that someone is implying a claim if in context it's clear that he believes the claim. In that case we infer that the person believes the claim.

I'm not going to vote, because no matter who is President nothing is going to get done about violence in the schools.
Evaluation An unstated claim is needed to make sense of what is said: "If no matter who is President nothing is going to get done about violence in the schools, then you shouldn't vote for President." We infer this from the person's remarks; he has implied it.

Instructor: My best students hand in extra-credit work.
Evaluation You might think the instructor is implying that you need to do extra-credit work to do well in the course. But she could say that you inferred incorrectly: She was just making an observation.

Instructor: You look terrific in that new outfit.
Evaluation: Is this sexual harassment? Be careful what you infer.

8 Compound Claims

> A *compound claim* is one that is composed of other claims, but has to be viewed as just one claim.

Either a Democrat will win the election or a Republican will win the election. *Compound.*

Either a Democrat or a Republican will win the election. *Compound.* (Rewrite this as the previous one.)

Suzy will pass her exam because she studied so hard. *Not compound.* This is an argument ("because" is an indicator).

> **Alternatives**   The claims that are parts of an "or" claim.

Dick or Zoe will go to the grocery to get eggs. *An "or" claim.* Alternatives: "Dick will go to the grocery to get eggs"; "Zoe will go the grocery to get eggs."

> **Contradictory of a Claim**   A *contradictory* of a claim is one that always has the opposite truth-value.

Spot barks. *Contradictory*: Spot does not bark.

Dick isn't a student. *Contradictory*: Dick is a student. (A contradictory needn't have "not" in it.)

Suzy will go to the movies or she will stay home. *Contradictory*: Suzy won't go to the movies and she won't stay home.

> ### Contradictory of an "or" Claim
> A or B *has contradictory* not A and not B.
>
> ### The Contradictory of an "and" Claim
> A and B *has contradictory* not A or not B.

Here "not A" means "the contradictory of A." The contradictory of "A or B" is also said as "Neither A, nor B."

Maria got the van or Manuel won't go to school.
Contradictory: Maria didn't get the van, and Manuel will go to school.

Tom or Suzy will pick up Manuel for class today.
Contradictory: Neither Tom nor Suzy will pick up Manuel for class today.

In order to present some valid forms of arguments using compound claims, we can let "A" and "B" stand for any claims, and a diagram with an arrow indicate "therefore."

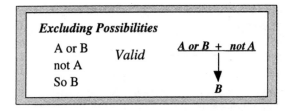

> ### Excluding Possibilities
> A or B
> not A   *Valid*
> So B

Either there is a wheelchair ramp at the school dance, or Manuel stayed home. But there isn't a wheelchair ramp at the school dance. Therefore, Manuel stayed home.

There can also be are more than two alternatives:

We can also exclude just some of the possibilities:

Either all criminals should be locked up forever, or we should put more money into rehabilitating criminals, or we should accept that our streets will never be safe, or we should have some system for monitoring ex-convicts. (*This is all one claim*: A or B or C or D.) We can't lock up all criminals forever, because it would be too expensive. We definitely won't accept that our streets will never be safe. So either we should put more money into rehabilitating criminals, or we should have some system for monitoring ex-convicts.

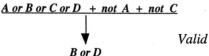

A or B or C or D + *not A* + *not C*

B or D   *Valid*

False dilemma   A bad use of excluding possibilities, where the "or" claim is false or implausible.

— Look at these bills! You're either going to have quit buying those nasty expensive cigars or get rid of Spot.
— What are you talking about? We can't get rid of Spot.
— So you agree, you'll give up smoking those cigars.
False dilemma. They could economize on dining out.

One type of compound claim is the conditional.

> ***Conditional Claim***   A claim that is or can be rewritten as an "if . . . then . . ." claim that must have the same truth-value.
>
> ***Antecedent and Consequent***   In a conditional (rewritten as) "If A, then B", the claim A is the *antecedent,* the claim B is the *consequent.*

If Spot ran away, then the gate was left open.
Conditional. Antecedent: "Spot ran away". Consequent: "The gate was left open." The consequent need not happen later.

I'll never talk to you again if you don't apologize.
Conditional. Antecedent: "You don't apologize."

Consequent: "I'll never talk to you again."

Bring me an ice cream cone and I'll be happy.
Conditional. Antecedent: "You bring me an ice cream cone."
Consequent: "I'll be happy."

Loving someone means you never throw dishes at them.
Conditional. Antecedent: "You love someone."
Consequent: "You never throw dishes at them."

Maria will not get AIDS since she is celibate now.
Not a conditional, not compound. Perhaps an argument, with
"since" introducing a single premise.

If Dick goes to the basketball game, then either he got a free ticket
or he borrowed money for one.
Conditional. Antecedent: "Dick goes to the basketball game."
Consequent: (another compound claim) "Dick got a free ticket or
he borrowed money for one."

Contradictory of a Conditional
If A, *then* B has contradictory A, *but not* B

If Spot barks, then Flo's cat will run away.
Contradictory: Spot barked, but Flo's cat did not run away.

If Spot got out of the yard, then he was chasing a squirrel.
Contradictory: Spot got out of the yard, but he wasn't chasing
a squirrel.

If cats had no fur, they would still give people allergies.
Contradictory: Even if cats had no fur, they would still give
people allergies. "Even if" is often used to make a contradictory
where there's a false antecedent—the "if" in it does not create a
conditional.

Bring me an ice cream cone and I'll be happy.
Contradictory: Despite that you brought me an ice cream cone,
I'm not happy. "Despite that" is used to make a contradictory, too.

The contradictory of a conditional is
not another conditional.

† If Suzy handed in all her homework in English, then she passed.

Contradictory: Suzy handed in all her homework in English, but she didn't pass.

Not contradictory: If Suzy didn't hand in all her homework in English, then she passed. (Both this and † could be true if Suzy passed regardless.)

Not contradictory: If Suzy handed in all her homework in English, then she didn't pass. (Both this and † could be true by default if Suzy didn't hand in all her homework.)

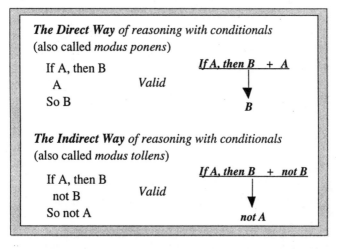

The Direct Way *of reasoning with conditionals*
(also called *modus ponens*)

If A, then B
A   *Valid*
So B

$\underline{If\ A, then\ B} + A$
$\downarrow$
B

The Indirect Way *of reasoning with conditionals*
(also called *modus tollens*)

If A, then B
not B   *Valid*
So not A

$\underline{If\ A, then\ B} + not\ B$
$\downarrow$
not A

Here, too, "not B" stands for "the contradictory of B."

If Spot barks, then Dick will wake up.
Spot barked.
So Dick woke up.
Valid, the direct way.

If Spot barks, then Dick will wake up.
Dick didn't wake up.
So Spot didn't bark.
Valid, the indirect way.

If Flo comes over to play,

If it's the day for the garbageman,

Then Dick will wake up.

If Suzy calls early,

If Spot barks,

If Suzy doesn't call early, then Zoe won't go shopping.
Zoe went shopping.
So Suzy called early.
Valid, the indirect way. The contradictory doesn't use "not".

Zoe won't go shopping if Dick comes home early.
Zoe went shopping.
So Dick didn't come home early.
Valid, the indirect way.

There are two forms of argument that are very similar to these valid forms but which are usually weak.

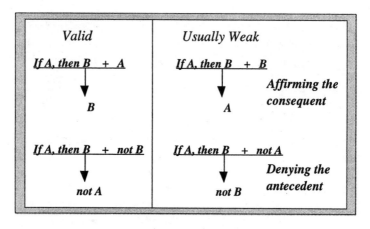

If Spot barks, then Dick will wake up.
Dick woke up.
So Spot barked.

Affirming the consequent. This is weak. Maybe Suzy called, or Flo came over to play. It's *reasoning backwards.*

If it's the day for the garbageman, then Dick will wake up.
It's not the day for the garbageman.
So Dick didn't wake up.

Denying the antecedent. Even though the garbageman didn't come, maybe Spot barked or Suzy called early. You can't overlook other possibilities. This, too, is reasoning backwards.

If Maria doesn't call Manuel, then Manuel will miss his class.
Maria did call Manuel.
So Manuel didn't miss his class.

Denying the antecedent. The "not" in the form indicates a contradictory. Schematically:

If <u>Maria doesn't call Manuel,</u> *then* <u>Manuel will miss his class.</u>
      A   B

<u>Maria did call Manuel</u>.   *So* <u>Manuel didn't miss his class.</u>
    not A   not B

These invalid forms of arguing are obvious confusions with valid forms, mistakes a good reasoner doesn't make. When you see one, *don't bother to repair the argument.*

If Suzy called early, then Dick woke up.
So Dick didn't wake up.
Evaluation The obvious premise to add is "Suzy didn't call early." But that makes the argument weak, so the argument is unrepairable.

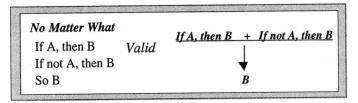

No Matter What		
If A, then B	*Valid*	If A, then B + If not A, then B
If not A, then B		↓
So B		B

Dick: If I study for my math exam this weekend we won't be able to have a good time at the beach.

Zoe: But if you don't study for your exam, you'll worry about it like you always do, and we won't have a good time at the beach. So it looks like this weekend is shot.

Contrapositive The *contrapositive* of "If A, then B" is "If not B, then not A." The contrapositive is true exactly when the original conditional is true.

If Spot barks, then Dick will wake up.
Contrapositive: If Dick doesn't wake up, then Spot didn't bark.
(See the picture on p. 37.)

A only if B *means the same as* If not B, then not A.

Via the contrapositive, "A only if B" is equivalent to "If A, then B." Though it may sound odd, *you can just replace* "only if" *by* "then." This is important in analyzing necessary and sufficient conditions.

All the following have the same truth-value:

> You can get a speeding ticket *only if* you are going over the speed limit.

> If you don't go over the speed limit, then you won't get a speeding ticket.

> If you get a speeding ticket, then you went over the speed limit.

What's necessary for getting a driver's license? You've got to pass the driving exam. That is, if you don't pass the driving exam, you won't get a driver's license. There's no way you'll get a driver's license if you don't pass the driver's exam. You'll get a driver's license *only if* you pass the driving exam.

What's sufficient for getting money at the bank? Cashing a check there will do. That is, if you cash a check at the bank, then you'll get money at the bank.

"A is *necessary* for B" means "If not A, then not B" is true.
"A is *sufficient* for B" means "If A, then B" is true.

So "A is necessary for B" just means that "B only if A" is true. Do not confuse "only if" with "if":

You can pass this course only if you study hard.

Analysis This isn't the same as "If you study hard, you can pass this course." Rather, studying hard is necessary, required to pass the course. It's not sufficient. Confusing "only if" with "if" is confusing necessary with sufficient conditions.

Reasoning in a chain is important. We go by little steps: if A, then B; if B, then C; ... Then if A is true, we can conclude the very last consequent.

If Dick takes Spot for a walk, then Zoe will cook dinner.
And if Zoe cooks dinner, then Dick will do the dishes.
So if Dick takes Spot for a walk, then he'll do the dishes.
But Dick did take Spot for a walk. So he must've done the dishes.

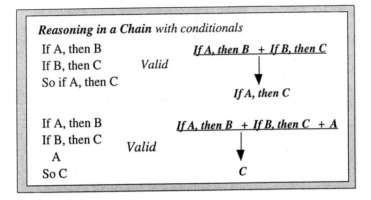

Reasoning in a Chain *with conditionals*

If A, then B	
If B, then C	*Valid*
So if A, then C	

$$\underline{\textit{If A, then B} \ + \ \textit{If B, then C}}$$
$$\downarrow$$
$$\textit{If A, then C}$$

If A, then B	
If B, then C	*Valid*
A	
So C	

$$\underline{\textit{If A, then B} \ + \ \textit{If B, then C} \ + \ A}$$
$$\downarrow$$
$$C$$

Slippery slope   A bad argument that uses a chain of conditionals, at least one of which is false or dubious.

Don't get a credit card! If you do, you'll be tempted to spend money you don't have. Then you'll max out on your card. Then you'll be in real debt. And you'll have to drop out of school to pay your bills. You'll end up a failure in life.
Slippery slope. You can see this by rewriting using conditionals.

Reasoning from Hypotheses   If you start with an assumption or hypothesis A that you don't know to be true and make a good argument for B, then what you have established is "If A, then B."

Lee: I'm thinking of majoring in biology.
Maria: That means you'll take summer school. Here's why:
        You're in your second year now. To finish in four years
        like you told me you need to, you'll have to take all the
        upper-division biology courses your last two years. And
        you can't take any of those until you've finished the three-
        semester calculus course. So you'll have to take calculus
        over the summer in order to finish in four years.

Maria has not proved that Lee has to go to summer school. Rather, on the assumption (hypothesis) that Lee will major in biology, Lee will have to go to summer school. That is, Maria has proved:
If Lee majors in biology, then he'll have to go to summer school.

9 Counterarguments

> Raising objections and answering them
> is part of making good arguments.

Dick: Zoe, we ought to get another dog.

Zoe: What's wrong with Spot?

Dick: Oh, no, I mean to keep Spot company.

Zoe: Spot has us. He doesn't need company.

Dick: But we're gone a lot. And he's always escaping from the yard, 'cause he's lonely. And we don't give him enough time. He should be out running around more.

Zoe: But think of all the work! We'll have to feed the new dog. And think of all the time necessary to train it.

Dick: I'll train him. We can feed him at the same time as Spot, and dog food is cheap. It won't cost much.

Dick is trying to convince Zoe to believe, "We should get another dog." But he has to answer her objections.

We ought to get another dog.

    (*objection*) We already have Spot.

The other dog will keep Spot company. (*answer*)

    (*objection*) Spot already has us for company.

We are gone a lot. (*answer*)

He is always escaping from the yard. (*answer*)

He's lonely. (*answer*)

We don't give him enough time. (*answer*)

He should be out running around more. (*answer*)

    (*objection*) It will be a lot of work to have a new dog.

    (*objection*) We will have to feed the new dog.

    (*objection*) It will take a lot of time to train the new dog.

I (Dick) will train him. (*answer*)

We can feed him at the same time as Spot. (*answer*)

Dog food is cheap. (*answer*)

Argument. Counterargument. Counter-counterargument. Objections are raised: Someone puts forward a claim that, if true, makes one of our claims false or at least doubtful. We then have to answer that challenge to sustain our argument. *Knocking off an objection is a mini-argument within your argument—if it's not a good (though brief) argument, it won't do the job.*

Or you could say, "I hadn't thought of that. I guess you're right."

Or you could say, "I don't know. I'll have to think about that."

In making an argument, you'll want to make it strong. You might think you have a great one. All the premises seem obvious and they glue together to get the conclusion. But if you imagine someone objecting, you can see how to give better support for doubtful premises. And answering counterarguments in your own writing allows the reader to see you haven't ignored some obvious objections. Just make a list of the pros and cons. Then answer the other side.

Direct Ways of Refuting an Argument
1. Show that at least one of the premises is false.
2. Show that the argument isn't valid or strong.
3. Show that the conclusion is false.

It's useless to kill flies. The ones you kill will be the slowest, because the fastest ones will evade you. Over time, then, the genes for being fast will predominate. Then with super-fast flies, it will be impossible to kill them anyway. So it's useless to kill flies.

To refute this argument: We might object to one of the premises, saying that you won't be killing the slowest ones, but only the ones that happen to come into your house.

Or we might accept the premises, but note that "over time" could be thousands of years, so the conclusion doesn't follow.

Or we could attack the conclusion directly, pointing out that we kill flies all the time and it keeps the house clean.

Reducing to the Absurd   To *reduce to the absurd* is to show that at least one of several claims is false or dubious, or collectively they are unacceptable, by drawing a false or unwanted conclusion from them.

You complain that taxes are already too high and there is too much crime. And you say we should permanently lock up everyone who has been convicted of three felonies. In the places where this has been instituted it hasn't reduced the crime rate. So we will have many, many more people who will be incarcerated for their entire lives. We will need more prisons, many more, because these people will be in forever. We will need to employ more guards. We will need to pay for a lot of health-care for these people when they are elderly. Thus, if you lock up everyone who has been convicted of three felonies, we will have to pay substantially higher taxes. Since you are adamant that taxes are too high, you should abandon your claim that we should permanently lock up everyone who has been convicted of three felonies.

Reducing to the absurd is an indirect way to refute an argument. If a valid argument has a false conclusion one of the premises is false. If a strong argument has a false conclusion, one of the premises is very likely false. If the conclusion is absurd, the premises aren't what you want.

Beware: Be sure the argument you use to get the false or absurd conclusion is strong or valid and doesn't use any other dubious claims. Only then do you have good reason to believe there's a problem with the original set of claims.

One way to reduce to the absurd is to use similar premises in an argument that sounds just like the original, yet leads to an absurd conclusion. This is refuting by analogy (see Chapter 11).

Look, your argument against killing flies is bad. We could use the same argument against killing bacteria, or against killing chickens for dinner from a farmer's henhouse. Those conclusions would be absurd.

Attempts to refute that are bad arguments

Phony refutations (pp. 17–18)

Slippery slope (p. 41)

Ridicule

Dr. E: I hear that your department elected a woman as chairman.

Professor Zzzyzzx: Jah, jah, dat is right. Und now ve is trying to decide vat we should be calling her—"chairman" or "chairwoman" or "chairperson."

Dr. E: "Chairperson"? Why not use a neutral term that's really appropriate for the position, like "chaircreature"?

No argument has been given for why "chairman" shouldn't be replaced by "chairperson," although Dr. E thinks he's shown that the idea is absurd. In rational discussion, ridicule is a device to end arguments, belittle your opponent, and make enemies.

Strawman A bad way to refute an argument by putting words in your opponent's mouth.

Tom: Unless we allow the logging of old-growth forests in this county, we'll lose the timber industry and these towns will die.

Dick: So you're saying that you don't care what happens to the spotted owl and to our rivers and the water we drink?

Tom: I said nothing of the sort. You've misrepresented my position.

The only reasonable response to a strawman is to say calmly that isn't what you said.

10 General Claims

We need to know how to reason with claims that are asserted about all, or some, or no things.

All means "Every single one, no exceptions." Sometimes *all* is meant as "Every single one, and there is at least one." Which reading is best may depend on the argument.

Some means "At least one." Sometimes *some* is meant as "At least one, but not all." Which reading is best may depend on the argument.

All dogs are mammals. *True.*

All dogs bark. *False*–on either reading of "all." ⟩ *How is it on the second reading?*

All polar bears in Antarctica can swim.
True–if you understand "all" as every single one. *False*–if you understand "all" to mean as well "at least one," since there aren't any polar bears in Antarctica.

Some dogs bark. *True*–on either reading of "some."

Some dogs are mammals.
True–if you understand "some" to mean just "at least one."
False–if you understand "some" to mean as well "and not all."

if you accept this then you are inferring that there are some that aren't which is false ???

Universal Claim   A claim that can be rewritten as an "all" claim that must have the same truth-value.

Existential Claim   A claim that can be rewritten as a "some" claim that must have the same truth-value.

The following universal claims all have the same truth-value:

All dogs bark.   Dogs bark.
Every dog barks.   Everything that's a dog barks.

The following existential claims all have the same truth-value:

Some dogs can't bark.   At least one dog can't bark.
There is a dog that can't bark.   There exists a dog that can't bark.

> **Negative Universal Claim**   A claim that can be
> rewritten as a "no" claim or an "all not" claim that
> must have the same truth-value.

The following negative universal claims have the same truth-value:

No dog likes cats.   Nothing that's a dog likes cats.
All dogs do not like cats.   Not even one dog likes cats.

> *Only* S are P   means   All P are S.

Only dogs bark.
Ralph is a dog.
So Ralph barks.

Not Valid. "Only dogs bark" does not mean that all dogs bark.
It means that anything that barks has got to be a dog.

Some examples of contradictories (p. 32) of general claims :

All dogs bark.
Contradictory: Some dogs don't bark.

Some dogs bark.
Contradictory: No dogs bark.

Some dogs don't bark.
Contradictory: All dogs bark.

No women are truck drivers.
Contradictory: Some women are truck drivers.

Every Mexican likes vodka.
Contradictory: Some Mexicans don't like vodka.

Some Russians like chili.
Contradictory: No Russian likes chili.

Some whales eat fish.
Contradictory: Not even one whale eats fish.

Only dogs bark.
Contradictory: Some things that bark are not dogs.

If we want to say that just exactly dogs bark and nothing else, we should say that, or "Dogs and only dogs bark." The contradictory of that is "Either some dogs don't bark, or some things that bark aren't dogs."

Given the many ways to make general claims, we have only a rough guide for how to form their contradictories:

Claim	*Contradictory*
All —	Some are not — Not every —
Some —	No — All are not — Not even one —
Some are not —	All are —
No —	Some are —
Only S are P	Some P are not S Not every P is S

It is easy to get confused whether an argument using a general claim is valid. There are some methods that can help us determine whether certain forms are valid or weak (see *Critical Thinking*.) Here are the most common valid forms, along with forms of weak arguments that are similar.

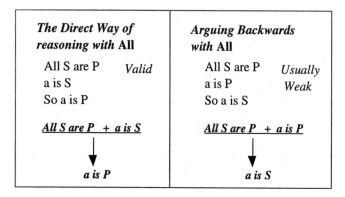

The Direct Way of reasoning with **All**	*Arguing Backwards with* **All**
All S are P *Valid* a is S So a is P	All S are P *Usually* a is P *Weak* So a is S
<u>*All S are P*</u> + *a is S* ↓ *a is P*	<u>*All S are P*</u> + *a is P* ↓ *a is S*

Valid: All dogs bark.   *Weak*:   All dogs bark.
           Ralph is a dog.   Ralph barks.
           So Ralph barks.   So Ralph is a dog.

The argument on the right is arguing backwards. One way to be something that barks is to be a dog, but there may be other ways (seals and foxes).

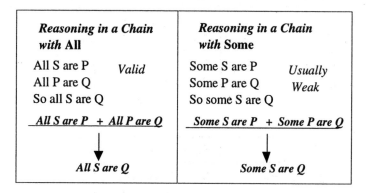

Reasoning in a Chain with **All**	*Reasoning in a Chain with* **Some**
All S are P *Valid* All P are Q So all S are Q	Some S are P *Usually* Some P are Q *Weak* So some S are Q
<u>*All S are P*</u> + *All P are Q* ↓ *All S are Q*	<u>*Some S are P*</u> + *Some P are Q* ↓ *Some S are Q*

Valid: All dogs bark.
           Everything that barks is a mammal.
           So all dogs are mammals.

Weak: Some cats are faithful to their owners.
           Some things that are faithful to their owners are dogs.
           Therefore, some cats are dogs.

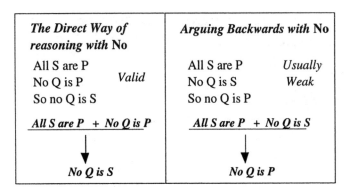

The Direct Way of reasoning with **No**	*Arguing Backwards with* **No**
All S are P	All S are P *Usually*
No Q is P *Valid*	No Q is S *Weak*
So no Q is S	So no Q is P
All S are P + No Q is P	*All S are P + No Q is S*
↓	↓
No Q is S	*No Q is P*

Valid: All dogs are mammals.   *Weak*:   All dogs bark.
No mammal lays eggs.   No fox is a dog.
So no dog lays eggs.   So no fox barks.

Precise generalities are easy to evaluate in arguments. For example:

72% of all workers at the GM plant say they will vote to strike. Harry works at the GM plant. So Harry will vote to strike.

Not strong. We can say exactly where this argument lands on the strong-weak scale: There's a 28% chance the premises could be true and conclusion false.

95% plus-or-minus 2% of all cat owners have cat-induced allergies. Dr. E's ex-wife has a cat. So very probably Dr. E's ex-wife has cat-induced allergies.

Strong. It's good if the premises are true.

Only 4% of all workers on the assembly line at the GM plant didn't get a raise last year. Wanda has worked on the assembly line at the GM plant since last year. So Wanda almost certainly got a raise.

Strong.

Vague generalities are difficult to reason with. They are usually too vague even to use in a claim. For example:

Most	Mostly	Many
A lot	Quite a lot	A bunch of
A few	A number of	

But two imprecise generalities are clear enough for us to use well in our reasoning:

Almost all   A very few

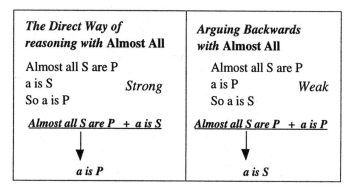

Almost all parakeets are under 2' tall.
So the parakeets at Boulevard Mall are under 2' tall.
Strong.

Almost all university professors teach every year.
Mary Jane teaches every year.
So Mary Jane is a university professor.
Weak. Mary Jane could be a high school teacher. Compare to arguing backwards with "all".

Reasoning in a chain with "almost all" is just as weak as reasoning in a chain with "some".

Almost all dogs like ice cream.
Almost all things that like ice cream don't bark.
So almost all dogs don't bark.
Weak.

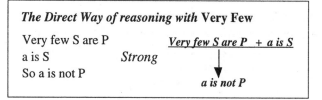

Very few cats are loyal.
Puff is a cat.
So Puff is not loyal.
Strong.

Comparable to the valid and weak forms using "no" are strong and weak forms using "a very few."

All S are P.   *Strong* Only a very few Q are P. So only a very few Q are S.

All truck drivers have a commercial driver's license.
Only a very few beauticians have a commercial driver's license.
So only a very few beauticians are truck drivers.
Strong.

All S are P.   *Weak* Only a very few Q are S. So only a very few Q are P.

All professors get a paycheck at the end of the month. Only a very few people under 25 are professors. So only a very few people under 25 get a paycheck at the end of the month. *Weak.*

Some of the following examples are applications of the forms above, but many are not. Often you just have to think your way through them. Remember, it's not whether the premises and conclusion happen to be true, but whether there are *possible* ways for the premises to be true and conclusion false.

Every newspaper that the Vice-President reads is published by an American publisher. All newspapers published by an American publisher are biased against Muslims. So the Vice-President reads only newspapers that are biased against Muslims.
Valid. Reasoning in a chain with "all".

Only managers can close out the cash register. George is a
manager. So George can close out the cash register.
Invalid and weak. "Only" does not mean "all". George could be
a manager in charge of the stock room.

Everyone who wants to become a manager works hard. The
people in Lois' group work hard. So the people in Lois' group
want to become managers.
Invalid and weak. Maybe the workers in Lois' group just want a
raise and not the responsibility. (A weak form: All S are Q; all P
are Q; therefore, all S are P.)

No taxpayer who cheats is honest. Some dishonest people are
found out. So some taxpayers who cheat are found out.
Invalid and weak. It could be that the only people who are found
out are ones who steal.

Not every truck driver gets speeding tickets. Kim is a truck driver.
So Kim doesn't get speeding tickets.
Invalid and weak.

Some dogs bite mailmen. Some mailmen bite dogs. So some dogs
and mailmen bite each other.
Invalid and weak. Maybe all the dogs who bite mailmen are
terrified of the mailmen who would bite them. So what, the statements don't talk about him terrified.

All lions are fierce, but some lions are afraid of dogs. So some dogs
aren't afraid of lions.
Invalid and weak. Maybe the dogs don't recognize that the lions
are afraid of them.

Some people who like pizza are vegetarians. Some vegetarians
will not eat eggs. So some people who like pizza will not eat eggs.
Invalid and weak. Even though all the premises and the conclusion are true, the argument is bad. This is reasoning in a chain with
"some".

No dogcatcher is kind. Anyone who's kind loves dogs. So no
dogcatcher loves dogs.
Invalid and weak. Arguing backwards with "no".

No students are enthusiastic about mathematics. Harry is enthusiastic about mathematics. So Harry is not a student.
Valid, though bad. The direct way of reasoning with "no".

All nursing students take critical thinking in their freshman year. No heroin addict is a nursing student. So no heroin addict takes critical thinking his freshman year.
Invalid and weak. Arguing backwards with "no".

Not every canary can sing. So some canaries can't sing.
Valid. If we read "every" to also mean "at least one."

Some nursing students aren't good at math. John is a nursing student. So John isn't good at math.
Invalid and weak. John could be one of the many nursing students who are good at math.

Every dog loves its master. Dick has a dog. So Dick is loved.
Valid.

Almost every dog loves its master. Dick has a dog. So Dick is loved.
Strong. A good argument.

Every cat sheds hair on its master's clothes. Dr. E does not have a cat. So Dr. E has no cat hair shed on his clothes.
Invalid and weak. Dr. E could have picked up cat hair visiting a friend who has a cat.

No one who reads this book is going to beg in the street. Because only poor people beg. And people who read this book won't be poor because they understand how to reason well. *Good!*

11 Analogies

A comparison becomes **reasoning by analogy** when it is part of an argument: On one side of the comparison we draw a conclusion, so on the other side we should conclude the same.

Should we let people who are HIV-positive remain in the military? Sure, after all, Magic Johnson is playing in the NBA.

Analogy. This is an argument: Magic Johnson is allowed to play in the NBA, so people who are HIV-positive should be allowed to remain in the military.

We should legalize marijuana. After all, if we don't, what's the rationale for making alcohol and tobacco legal?

Analogy. Alcohol is legal. Tobacco is legal. Therefore, marijuana should be legal. They are sufficiently similar.

DDT has been shown to cause cancer in rats. Therefore, there is a good chance DDT will cause cancer in humans.

Analogy. Rats are like humans. So if rats get cancer from DDT, so will humans.

My love is like a red, red rose.

Not reasoning by analogy. What conclusion is being drawn?

An analogy is usually a weak argument. It will rely on an implicit, unstated general principle. The value of the analogy will be to force us to try to make that principle explicit.

"Blaming soldiers for war is like blaming firemen for fires."

(Background: Country Joe MacDonald was a rock star who wrote songs protesting the war in Vietnam. In 1995 he was interviewed on National Public Radio about his motives for working to establish a memorial for Vietnam War soldiers in Berkeley, California, his home and a center of anti-war protests in the 60s and 70s. This claim was his response.)

Evaluation This is a comparison. But it's meant as an argument:

> We don't blame firemen for fires.
> Firemen and fires are like soldiers and wars.
> Therefore, we should not blame soldiers for war.

In what way are firemen and fires like soldiers and wars? They have to be similar enough in some respect for Country Joe's remark to be more than suggestive. We need to pick out important similarities that we can use as premises.

> *Firemen and fires are like soldiers and war.*
> wear uniforms
> answer to chain of command
> cannot disobey superior without serious consequences
> fight (fires/wars)
> work done when fire/war is over
> until recently only men
> lives at risk in work
> fire/war kills others
> firemen don't start fires—soldiers don't start wars
> usually like beer

That's stupid: Firemen and soldiers usually like beer. So?

When you ask "So?" you're on the way to deciding if the analogy is good. It's not just any similarity that's important. There must be some crucial, important way that firemen fighting fires is like soldiers fighting wars, some similarity that can account for why we don't blame firemen for fires that also applies to soldiers and war. Some of the similarities listed don't seem to matter. Others we can't use because they trade on an ambiguity, like saying firemen "fight" fires.

We don't have any good guide for how to proceed—that's a

weakness of the original argument. But if we are to take Country Joe MacDonald's remark seriously, we have to come up with some principle that applies to both sides.

The similarities that seem most important are that both firemen and soldiers are involved in dangerous work, trying to end a problem/disaster they didn't start. We don't want to blame someone for helping to end a disaster that could harm us all.

(‡) Firemen are involved in dangerous work.
Soldiers are involved in dangerous work.
The job of a fireman is to end a fire.
The job of a soldier is to end a war.
Firemen don't start fires.
Soldiers don't start wars.

But even with these added to the original argument, we don't get a good argument for the conclusion that we shouldn't blame soldiers for wars. We need a general principle:

You shouldn't blame someone for helping to end a disaster that could harm others, if he didn't start the disaster.

This general principle seems plausible, and it yields a valid argument.

But is the argument good? Are all the premises true? This is the point where the differences between firemen and soldiers might be important.

The first two premises of (‡) are clearly true, and so is the third. But is the job of soldiers to end a war? And do soldiers really not start wars? Look at this difference:

Without firemen there would still be fires.
Without soldiers there wouldn't be any wars.

Without soldiers there would still be violence. But without soldiers—any soldiers anywhere—there could be no organized violence of one country against another ("What if they gave a war and nobody came?").

So? The analogy shouldn't convince. The argument has a dubious premise.

We did not prove that soldiers should be blamed for wars. As always, *when you show an argument is bad you haven't proved the conclusion false.* You've only shown that you have no more reason than before for believing the conclusion.

Perhaps the premises at (‡) could be modified, using that soldiers are drafted for wars. But that's beyond Country Joe's argument. If he meant something more, then it's his responsibility to flesh it out. Or we could use his comparison as a starting place to decide whether there is a general principle, based on the similarities, for why we shouldn't blame soldiers for war.

Evaluating an Analogy

1. Is this an argument? What is the conclusion?
2. What is the comparison?
3. What are the premises (the sides of the comparison)?
4. What are the similarities?
5. Can we state the similarities as premises and find a general principle that covers the two sides?
6. Does the general principle really apply to both sides? What about the differences?
7. Is the argument strong or valid? Is it good?

The basic pattern of legal reasoning is reasoning by example. It is reasoning from case to case. It is a three-step process described by the doctrine of precedent in which a proposition descriptive of the first case is made into a rule of law and then applied to a next similar situation. The steps are these: similarity is seen between cases; next the rule of law inherent in the first case is announced; then the rule of law is made applicable to the second case.

         Edward H. Levi, *An Introduction to Legal Reasoning*

12 Models

Models in science are used for reasoning by analogy: We can draw conclusions based on the similarities, so long as the differences don't matter.

Here is an accurate map of Minersville, Utah:

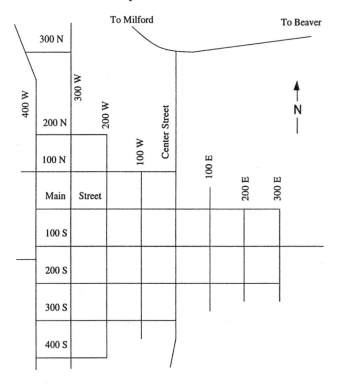

We can see from this that the streets are evenly spaced, for example, there is the same distance between 100 N and 200 N as between 100 E and 200 E. The last street to the east is 300 E.

There is no paved road going north beyond Main St. on 200 E.

That is, from this map we can deduce claims about Minersville, even if we've never been there. But there is much we can't deduce: Are there hills in Minersville? Are there lots of trees? How wide are the streets? How far apart are the streets? Where are there houses? The map is accurate for what it pays attention to: the relative location of streets. But it tells us nothing about what it ignores.

Reasoning about Minersville from this map is reasoning by analogy. The map is similar to Minersville in the relative position of streets and their orientation to North. The differences between the map and Minersville aren't important when we infer that the north end of 200 W is at 200 N. Perhaps you've seen scale models of terrain, a scale model of a city or a mountain. Such a model abstracts less from the actual terrain: height and perhaps placements of rivers and trees are there.

A model ***models more*** than another if there are more similarities between the model and what it's modeling. The map of Minersville ***abstracts more*** from the actual terrain than a scale model of the city does—that is, it ignores more. *We can use a model only to deduce claims based on the similarities, where the differences don't matter.*

> When scientists are trying to understand a particular set of phenomena, they often make use of a *model*. A model, in the scientists' sense, is a kind of analogy or mental image of the phenomena in terms of something we are familiar with. One example is the wave model of light. We cannot see waves of light as we can see water waves; but it is valuable to think of light as if it were made up of waves because experiments on light indicate that it behaves in many respects as water waves do.
>
> The purpose of a model is to give us a mental or visual picture—something to hold onto—when we cannot see what is actually happening. Models often give us a deeper understanding: the analogy to a known system (for instance, water waves in the above example) can suggest new experiments to perform and can provide ideas about what

other related phenomena might occur.

D. C. Giancoli, *Physics,* 2nd edition, p. 4.

Models in science can be merely suggestive, suggesting claims to investigate or suggesting relationships that might hold. Or models can be as precise as the map of Minersville and just as reliable if we are careful to pay attention to what similarities they depend on and what differences are important.

Models of the atom

The atomic model of matter has gone through many refinements. At one time or another, atoms were imagined to be tiny spheres with hooks on them (to explain chemical bonding), or as tiny billiard balls continually bouncing against each other. More recently, the "planetary model" of the atom visualized the atom as a nucleus with electrons revolving around it, just as the planets revolve around the sun.

D. C. Giancoli, *Physics,* 2nd edition, p. 4.

Analysis Giancoli describes various models of the atom as they were used to help visualize the working of something we can't see. What isn't mentioned, however, are all the other claims about the workings of the atom that were made in conjunction with those pictures, claims from which predictions about the behavior of chemical compounds could be made. Those claims, along with the similarities between atoms and the models that were proposed, constituted the atomic theory of that time.

The kinetic model of gases

This theory is based on the following postulates, or assumptions.

1. Gases are composed of a large number of particles that behave like hard, spherical objects in a state of constant, random motion.
2. The particles move in a straight line until they collide with another particle or the walls of the container.
3. The particles are much smaller than the distance between the particles. Most of the volume of a gas is therefore empty space.

4. There is no force of attraction between gas particles or between the particles and the walls of the container.

5. Collisions between gas particles or collisions with the walls of the container are perfectly elastic. Energy can be transferred from one particle to another during a collision, but the total kinetic energy of the particles after the collision is the same as it was before the collision.

6. The average kinetic energy of a collection of gas particles depends on the temperature of the gas and nothing else.

J. Spencer, G. Bodner, and L. Rickard, *Chemistry*.

Analysis Here is a picture of what is supposed to be going on in a gas in a closed container.

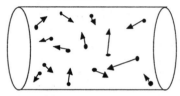

The molecules of gas are represented as dots, as if they were hard spherical balls. The length of the line emanating from a particle models the particle's speed; the arrow models the direction the particle is moving. The kinetic energy of a particle is defined in terms of its mass and velocity: kinetic energy = $.5 \, mv^2$.

The model defines what is meant for a collision to be elastic, but for comparison, here is a picture of what happens in an inelastic collision between a rubber ball and a floor:

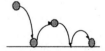

Each time the ball hits the ground, some of its kinetic energy is lost through being transferred to the floor or in compressing the ball.

The kinetic model of gases abstracts very much from what a gas in a container actually is: Molecules of gas are not generally spherical and are certainly not solid; the collisions between molecules and the walls of a container or each other are not perfectly elastic; there is some gravitational attraction between the particles and each other and also with the container. That is, there are a lot of differences.

But are there enough similarities for the model to be useful? The pressure of a gas results from the collisions between the gas particles and the walls of the container. So if the container is made smaller and all else remains the same, the pressure should increase; and vice-versa, if the container is made larger, the pressure should be less. Thus, the pressure should be proportional to the inverse of the volume of the gas. That is, the model suggests a claim about the relationship of pressure to volume in a gas. Experiments have been performed, varying the pressure or volume, and they are all close to being in accord with that claim.

Other laws are also suggested by the model: Pressure is proportional to the temperature of the gas, where the temperature is supposed to be the average kinetic energy of the gas. The volume of the gas should be proportional to the temperature. The amount of gas should be proportional to the pressure. All of these are confirmed by experiment.

Those experiments confirming predictions from the model do not mean that the model is more accurate than we thought. Collisions still aren't really elastic; molecules aren't really hard spherical balls. As in any analogy: *We can use the similarities to draw conclusions, so long as the differences don't matter.*

The acceleration of falling objects

Analysis Galileo argued that falling objects accelerate as they fall: They begin falling slowly and fall faster and faster the farther they fall. He didn't need any mathematics in that argument. He just noted that a heavy stone dropped from 6 feet will drive a stake into the ground much farther than if it were dropped from 6 inches.

But Galileo went further. He said the reason that a feather falls more slowly than an iron ball when dropped is because of the resistance of air. He argued that at a given location on the earth and in the absence of air resistance, all objects should fall with the same acceleration. He claimed that the distance traveled by a falling object is proportional to the square of the time it travels, $d \propto t^2$. Today, from many measurements, the equation is given by:

‡) $\qquad d = 9.80 \text{ meters} / \text{sec}^2 \cdot t^2$

$\qquad d$ is distance measured in meters; t is time in seconds

Equation (‡) is very precise; with it we can make calculations. For example, if you drop a ball from the Empire State Building, after 4 seconds it should have traveled:

$$d = 9.80 \text{ m}_{/\text{sec}}2 \cdot (4 \text{ sec})^2 = 9.80 \text{ m} \cdot 16$$

$$= 156.8 \text{ m} \qquad \text{about } 517.5 \text{ feet}$$

In what sense is equation (‡) an analogy? It says that if we compare a falling object to an imaginary point mass falling to the earth with no air resistance, any calculation (which is really a deduction) that holds from the equation also will hold for the object. The differences don't matter. Or rather, they don't matter very much, since air resistance does slow down an object. Indeed, if an object falls far enough, say if you drop a stuffed toy cat from an airplane, it will reach a maximum velocity when the force of the air resistance equals the acceleration. And it matters where on earth you are: An object dropped from a 100 foot building in San Francisco will accelerate more than an object dropped from a 100 foot building in Denver, which is 5000 feet above sea level.

The mass of the object being dropped doesn't matter, too, because the results of the calculations using (‡) will be close enough for most of our purposes. But we can't use (‡) for calculating how the moon moves relative to the Earth, because the differences do matter: The moon has a mass that is large enough compared to the earth to be significant.

Mathematical equations can be understood as analogies, because we can draw conclusions from them (use them to calculate) when the differences don't matter.

13 Numbers

We use numbers to be exact, but it's easy to be misled when reasoning with them.

A vague or meaningless comparison gets no better by having a few numbers in it—that's *apples and oranges*.

There were twice as many rapes as murders in our town.
Evaluation This seems to say something important, but what?

It's getting really violent here. There were 12% more murders this year than last.
Evaluation This is a mistaken comparison. If the town is growing rapidly and the number of tourists is growing even faster, it would be no surprise that the *number* of murders is going up, though the *rate* (how many murders per 100,000 population) might be going down. It's safer to live in a town of one million that had 20 murders last year than in a small town of 25,000 that had 6.

> *Two Times Zero Is Still Zero*   A comparison that makes something look impressive, but the base of the comparison is not stated.

A clothing store advertises a sale of sweaters at "25% off." You take it to mean 25% off the price they used to charge which was $20, so you'd pay $15. But the store could mean 25% off the suggested retail price of $26, so it's now $19.50. You have to ask "25% off *what?*"

Percentages can be misleading. For example:

Tom sees a stock for $60 and think it's a good deal. He buys it; a week later it's at $90, so he sells. He made $30—a 50% gain! His friend Wanda hears about it and buys the stock at $90; a week later it goes down to $60, so she panics and sells the stock. Wanda lost $30—that's a $33\frac{1}{3}$% loss. The same $30 is a different percentage depending on where you started.

$$50\% \uparrow \left[\begin{array}{c} \$90 \\ \$60 \end{array} \right] \downarrow 33\frac{1}{3}\%$$

Often numbers are cited where it is clear *there is no way the number could be known.*

National Public Radio: "Breast feeding is up 16% from 1989."
Evaluation How could they know? Who was looking in all those homes? A survey? Whom did they ask? Women chosen randomly? But lots of them don't have infants. Women who visited doctors? But lots of women, lots of poor ones, don't visit their doctors. What does "breast feeding" mean? Does a woman who breast feeds one day and then gives it up classify as someone who breast feeds? Or one who breast feeds two days? A month?
    Maybe NPR is reporting on a reliable survey. But what they said is so vague and open to doubt as to how they could know it that we should ignore it as noise.

> **Mean, median, and mode**
> The **average** or **mean** of a collection of numbers is
>   obtained by adding the numbers and then
>   dividing by the number of items.
> The **median** is the midway mark: the same number
>   of items above as below.
> The **mode** is the number most often attained.

The *average* of 7, 9, 37, 22, 109, 9, 11 is calculated:
    Add $7 + 9 + 37 + 22 + 109 + 9 + 11 = 204$
    Divide 204 by 7 = 29.14, the average
The *median* is 11.
The *mode* is 9

An average is a useful figure to know only if there isn't too much variation in the figures. For example:

Dr. E's Final Exam

score	number of students
95	3 students
94	7 students
92	1 student
90	4 students
75	1 student
62	4 students
57	5 students
55	4 students
52	2 students

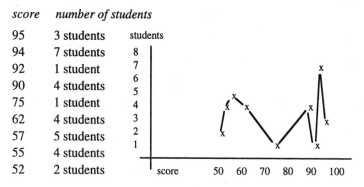

The grading scale was 90–100 = A, 80–89 = B, 70–79 = C, 60–69 = D, 59 and below = F. When Dr. E's department head asked him how the teaching went, he told her, "Great, just like you wanted, the average mark was 75%, a C." But she knows Dr. E too well to be satisfied. She asks him, "What was the median score?" Again Dr. E can reply, "75." As many got above 75 as below 75. But knowing how clever Dr. E is with numbers, she asks him what the mode score was. Dr. E flushes, "Well, 94." Now she knows something is fishy. When she wanted the average score to be about 75, she was thinking of a graph that looked like:

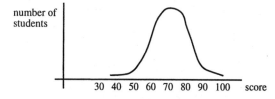

The distribution of the marks should be in a bell-shape: clustered around the median.

Unless you have good reason to believe that the average mark is pretty close to the median and that the distribution is more or less bell-shaped, the average doesn't tell you anything important.

14 Generalizing

We generalize every day, arguing from
a claim about some to a claim about more.

> **Generalizing** We are *generalizing* if we conclude a
> claim about a group, the ***population***, from a claim
> about some part of it, the ***sample***. To generalize is to
> make an argument.
>
> Sometimes the general claim that is the conclusion
> is called the ***generalization***; sometimes we call the
> whole argument a generalization.
>
> The claims about the sample are called the
> ***inductive evidence*** for the generalization.

When we generalize from experience we cannot be certain of our conclusions. At best we can get a strong argument.

In a study of 5,000 people who owned pets in Anchorage, Alaska, dog owners expressed higher satisfaction with their pets and with their own lives. So dog owners are more satisfied with their pets and their own lives than other pet owners.

Sample: The 5,000 people who were surveyed in Anchorage.
Population: Pet owners everywhere.

Of potential customers surveyed, 72% said that they liked "very much" the new green color that Yoda plans to use for its cars. So about 72% of all potential customers will like it.

Sample: The group of potential customers interviewed.
Population: All potential customers.
This is a *statistical generalization*.

Every time the minimum wage is raised, there's squawking that it will cause inflation and decrease employment. And every time it doesn't. So watch for the same bad arguments again this time.

Evaluation   The unstated conclusion is that raising the minimum wage will not cause inflation or decrease employment. This is a generalization from the past to the future. *Sample:* All times in the past that the minimum wage has risen. *Population*: All times it has risen or will rise.

The doctor tells you to fast from 10 p.m. At 10 a.m. she gives you glucose to drink. Forty-five minutes later she takes some of your blood and has it analyzed. She concludes you don't have diabetes.
Sample: The blood the doctor took.
Population: All the blood you have in your body.

Wanda goes to the city council meeting with a petition signed by all the people who live on her block requesting that a street light be put in. Addressing the city council, she says, "Everyone on this block wants a street light here."
Not a generalization. There's no argument from some to more, since the sample equals the population.

> ***Representative Sample***   A sample in which no one subgroup of the whole population is represented more than its proportion in the population.
>   A sample is ***biased*** if it is not representative.

Haphazard sampling   Choosing the sample with no intentional bias. It may result in a representative sample, but we won't have any good reason to believe that the sample is representative.

To determine the attitudes of students about sex before marriage, Tom and three friends give a questionnaire to the first 20 students they meet coming out of the student union, the administration offices, and the largest classroom building at 9 a.m., 1 p.m., and 6 p.m. They are choosing a sample of students haphazardly. There is no reason to think the sample is representative.

> ***Random Sampling*** A sample is chosen *randomly* if at every choice there is an equal chance for any one of the remaining members of the population to be picked.

If Tom assigns a number to each student, writes the numbers on slips of paper, puts them in a fishbowl, and draws one number at a time, that's probably going to be a random selection. But there's a chance that slips with longer numbers will have more ink and fall to the bottom of the bowl when you shake it. Or the slips aren't all the same size. So typically to get a random selection we use tables of random numbers prepared by mathematicians. Most spreadsheet programs for home computers can generate tables of random numbers. For Tom's survey he could get a list of all students; if the first number on the table is 413 he'd pick the 413th student on the list; if the second number is 711, he'd pick the 711th student on the list; and so on, until he has a sample that's big enough.

Random sampling is very likely going to yield a sample that is representative.

Suppose that of the 20,000 students at your school, 500 are gay males. Then the chance that *one* student picked at random would be a gay male is: $\frac{500}{20,000} = \frac{1}{40}$. If you were to pick 300 students at random, the chance that half of them would be gay is very, very small. It is very likely, however, that 7 or 8 ($1/40$ of 300) will be gay males.

On the other hand, suppose roughly 50% of the students at your school are female. Then each time you choose a student at random there's a 50% chance it will be female. And if you randomly choose a sample of 300 students the chance is very high that close to 50% will be female.

The ***law of large numbers*** says, roughly, that if the probability of something occurring is X percent, then over the long run the percentage of times that happens will be about X percent.

The probability of a flip of a fair coin landing heads is 50%. So although you may get a run of 8 tails, then 5 heads, then 4 tails, then 36 heads to start, in the long run, repeating the flipping, if the coin is fair, eventually the number of heads will tend toward 50%.

The gambler's fallacy A bad argument that a run of events of a certain kind makes a run of contrary events more likely in order to even up the probabilities.

Dick (at a roulette table): It's come up red 12 times in a row. It's bound to come up black several times in a row now.
Wrong. It could come up red 100 times in a row, and black could even out by coming up just one more time than red every 100 spins for the next 10,000 spins.

If you choose a large sample randomly, the chance is very high that it will be representative. That's because the chance of any one subgroup being over-represented is small—not nonexistent, but small. It doesn't matter if you know anything about the composition of the population in advance. After all, to know how many homosexuals there are, and how many married women, and how many men, and . . . you'd need to know almost everything about the population in advance. But that's what you use surveys to find out.

With a random sample we have good reason to believe the sample is representative. A sample chosen haphazardly may give a representative sample—but you have no good reason to believe it will be representative.

Weak Argument	*Strong Argument*
Sample is chosen *haphazardly*. Therefore, the sample is representative.	Sample is chosen *randomly*. Therefore, the sample is representative.
Lots of ways the sample could be biased.	Low probability the sample could be biased.

The classic example that haphazard sampling can be bad, even with an enormous sample, is the poll done in 1936 by *Literary*

Digest. The magazine mailed out 10,000,000 ballots asking who the person would vote for in the 1936 presidential election. They received 2,300,000 back. With that huge sample, the magazine confidently predicted that Alf Landon would win. Roosevelt received 60% of the vote, one of the biggest wins ever. What went wrong? The magazine selected its sample from lists of its own subscribers and telephone and automobile owners. In 1936 that was the wealthy class, which preferred Alf Landon.

Three premises are necessary, though not sufficient, for a generalization to be good.

Premises for a Good Generalization
The sample is representative.
The sample is big enough.
The sample is studied well.
    Therefore: Generalization.

Sample Size The sample has to be big enough for a generalization to be good. Generalizing from a sample that is too small is called a *hasty generalization* or *anecdotal evidence*.

I've got a couple of Chinese students in my classes. They're both hard-working and get good grades. All Chinese must be like that.

How big does a sample have to be? Roughly, the idea is to measure how much more likely it is that your generalization is going to be accurate as you increase the number in your sample. If you want to find out how many people in your class of 300 sociology students are spending 10 hours a week on the homework, you might ask 15 or 20. If you interview 30 you might get a better picture, but there's a limit. After you've asked 100, you probably won't get a much different result if you ask 150. And if you've asked 200, do you really think your generalization will be different if you ask 250? It hardly seems worth the effort.

Often you can rely on common sense when small numbers are involved. But when we generalize to a very large population, say 2,500, or 25,000, or 250,000,000, how big the sample should be cannot be explained without at least a mini-course on statistics. In evaluating statistical generalizations, you have to expect that the people doing the sampling have looked at enough examples, which is reasonable if it's a respected organization, a well-known polling company, physicians, or a drug company that's got to answer to the Food and Drug Administration. Surprisingly, perhaps, 1,500 is typically adequate for the sample size when surveying all adults in the U.S.

However, how big the sample has to be depends on how much *variation* there is in the population. If there is very little variation, then a small sample chosen haphazardly will do. Lots of variation (or where you don't know how much variation there is) demands a very large sample, and random sampling is the best way to get a representative sample.

It's incredible how much information they can put on a CD. I just bought one that contains a whole encyclopedia.

Good generalization. Unstated conclusion: Every CD can contain as much information as this one that has an encyclopedia on it. There is little variation in the production of CDs for computers; a sample of one is sufficient.

The Sample is Studied Well   The doctor taking your blood to see if you have diabetes won't get a reliable result if her syringe is contaminated or if she forgets to tell you to fast the night before. You won't find out the attitudes of students about sex before marriage if you ask a biased question. Picking a random sample of bolts won't help you determine if the bolts are O.K. if all you do is inspect them visually, not with a microscope or a stress test.

Questionnaires and surveys are particularly problematic. Questions need to be formulated without bias. Even then, you have to rely on the respondents answering truthfully.

Surveys on sexual habits are notorious for inaccurate reporting. Invariably the number of times that women in the U.S. report they engaged in sexual intercourse with a man in the last week, or month, or year is much lower than the reports that men give of sexual intercourse with a woman during that time. The figures are so different that it would be impossible for both groups to be answering accurately.

The Margin of Error and the Confidence Level   It's never reasonable to believe exact statistical generalizations: 37% of the people in your town who were surveyed wear glasses, so 37% of all people in your town wear glasses. No matter how many people in your town are surveyed, short of virtually all of them, you can't be confident that exactly 37% of all of them wear glasses. Rather, "37%, more or less, wear glasses" would be the right conclusion.

That "more or less" can be made fairly precise according to a theory of statistics. The ***margin of error*** gives the range within which the actual number for the population is likely to fall. For example:

The opinion poll says that when voters were asked their preference, the incumbent was favored by 53% and the challenger by 47%, with a margin of error of 2%, and a confidence level of 95%. So the incumbent will win tomorrow.

From this survey they are concluding that the percentage of *all* voters who favor the incumbent is between 51% and 55%, while the challenger is favored by between 45% and 49%. The ***confidence level*** measures how likely it is that they're right. The confidence level here is 95%, which means that there is a 95% chance it's true that the actual percentage of voters who prefer the incumbent is between 51% and 55%. If the confidence level were 70%, then the survey wouldn't be very reliable: There would be a 3-out-of-10 chance the conclusion is false. Typically, if the confidence level is below 95%, the results won't be announced.

The bigger the sample, the higher the confidence level and the lower the margin of error. The problem is to decide how much it's worth in extra time and expense to increase the sample size in order to get a stronger argument.

Risk Risk doesn't change how strong an argument you have, only how strong an argument you want before you'll accept the conclusion.

With a shipment of 30 bolts, inspecting 5 and finding them O.K. would allow you to conclude that all the bolts are O.K. But if they're for the space shuttle, where a bad bolt could doom the spacecraft, you'd want to inspect each and every one of them.

Selective attention We can be misled by how we pay attention.

It seems that buttered toast always lands the wrong side down, because you notice it when it does.

Examples

Every time I've seen a stranger come to Dick's gate, Spot has barked. So Spot will always bark at strangers at Dick's gate.

Bad generalization. The sample is haphazard. There's no reason to believe it's representative.

In a study of 5,000 people who owned pets in Anchorage, Alaska, dog owners expressed higher satisfaction with their pets and their lives. So dog owners are more satisfied with their pets and their own lives.

Bad generalization. The sample is clearly not representative. At best the evidence could lead to a conclusion about all pet owners in Anchorage, Alaska.

Maria has asked all but three of the thirty-six people in her class whether they've ever used heroin. Only two said "yes." So Maria concludes that almost no one in the class has used heroin.

Bad generalization. The sample is big enough and representative, but not studied well. People are not likely to admit to a stranger that they've used heroin; an anonymous questionnaire is needed.

My grandmother was diagnosed with cancer seven years ago. She refused any treatment that was offered to her over the years. She's perfectly healthy and doing great. The treatment for cancer is just a scam to get people's money.

Bad generalization. It's just anecdotal evidence.

Dick: A study I read said people with large hands are better at math.

Suzy: I guess that explains why I can't divide.

Bad application of a generalization. Perhaps the study was done carefully with a random sample. But you don't need a study to know that people with large hands do better at math: Babies have smaller hands, and they can't even add. *All people* is the wrong population to study.

Of chimpanzees fed one pound of chocolate per day in addition to their usual diet, 72% became obese within two months. Therefore, it is likely that most humans who eat 2% of their body weight in chocolate daily will become obese within two months.

Analogy. A generalization is needed to make this analogy good: 72% of *all* chimpanzees, more or less, will become obese if fed one pound of chocolate per day in addition to their usual diet. Whether this is a good generalization will depend on whether the researchers can claim that their sample is representative. The analogy then needs a claim about the similarity of chimpanzee physiology to human physiology.

15 Cause and Effect

We can establish guidelines for how to reason about cause and effect.

What exactly is a *cause*? Consider what Dick said last night,

> Spot caused me to wake up.

Spot is the thing that somehow caused Dick to wake up. But it's not just that Spot existed. It's what he was doing that caused Dick to wake up:

Spot's barking caused Dick to wake up.

So Spot's barking is the cause? What kind of thing is that? The easiest way to describe the cause is to say:

> Spot barked.

The easiest way to describe the effect is to say:

> Dick woke up.

Causes and effects can be described with claims.

This allows us to use all we know about claims in the analysis of cause and effect, for instance whether they are objective or subjective, and whether a sentence is too vague to describe a cause or effect.

A *causal claim* is a claim that can be rewritten in the form "A causes (caused) B." For example, "Spot caused

Dick to wake up" is a ***particular cause and effect*** (causal claim). This happened once, then that happened.

We could generalize from this particular cause and effect to: "Very loud barking by someone's dog near him when he is sleeping *causes* him to wake, if he's not deaf." This is a ***general cause and effect*** claim. For it to be true, lots of particular cause and effect claims must be true.

The police car's siren got me to pull over.
Particular causal claim. Cause: The police car had its siren going. Effect: I pulled over.

Because you were late, we missed the beginning of the movie.
Particular causal claim. Cause: You were late. Effect: We missed the beginning of the movie.

Penicillin prevents serious infection.
Too vague. What is the cause? The existence of penicillin? It's that penicillin is administered to people in certain amounts at certain stages of their infections. Further, what's a "serious infection"? This is too vague to count as a causal claim.

Drinking coffee keeps people awake.
General causal claim. Cause: People drink coffee. Effect: People stay awake. Perhaps too vague.

What must be true for there to be cause and effect?

The cause and effect happened Both the cause and effect have to be described by claims that are true. We wouldn't say that Spot's barking caused Dick to wake up if either Dick didn't wake up or Spot didn't bark.

It's (nearly) impossible for the cause to happen and the effect not to happen It can't be just coincidence that Dick woke up when Spot barked. It has to be (nearly) impossible for the claim describing the cause to be true and the claim describing the effect to be false.

That's just the relation of premises to conclusion in a valid or strong argument. Only here we're not trying to convince anyone that the conclusion is true: We know that Dick woke up. What we can carry over from our study of arguments is how to look for all the possibilities—all the ways the premises could be true and conclusion false—to determine if there is cause and effect.

But the cause by itself is almost never enough to ensure that the effect follows.

A lot has to be true for it to be impossible for "Spot barked" to be true and "Dick woke up" to be false:

> Dick was sleeping soundly up to the time that Spot barked.
> Spot barked at 3 a.m.
> Spot was close to where Dick was sleeping. . . .

We could go on forever. But as with arguments, we state what we think is important and leave out the obvious. If someone challenged us, we could add "There was no earthquake at the time"—but we just assume that.

The obvious unstated claims that are needed to establish cause and effect, comparable to unstated premises for an argument, are called the *normal conditions*. We can take claims as normal conditions only if they are obviously true and make the inference valid or strong.

For a general causal claim, such as "Very loud barking by someone's dog near him when he is sleeping *causes* him to wake, if he's not deaf," the normal conditions won't be specific just to the one time Spot woke Dick, but will be general.

The cause precedes the effect We wouldn't accept that Spot's barking caused Dick to wake up if Spot began barking only after Dick woke up. The cause has to precede the effect. That is, "Spot barked" became true before "Dick woke up" became true. For there to be cause and effect, the cause has to become true before the effect becomes true.

The cause makes a difference Dr. E has a desperate fear of elephants. So he buys a special wind chime and puts it outside his door to keep the elephants away. He lives in Cedar City, Utah, at 6,000 feet above sea level in a desert, and he confidently claims that the wind chime causes the elephants to stay away. After all, ever since he put up the wind chime he hasn't seen any elephants.

Why are we sure the wind chime being up did *not* cause elephants to stay away? Because even if there had been no wind chime, the elephants would have stayed away. Which elephants? All elephants. The wind chime works, but so would anything else. The wind chime doesn't make a difference. *For there to be cause and effect, it must be that if there were no cause, there would be no effect.* If Spot had not barked, Dick would not have woken up.

There is no common cause We don't say that night causes day, because there is a common cause of both "It was night" and "It is now day," namely, "The earth is rotating relative to the sun." For there to be cause and effect, there must be no common cause.

Dick: Zoe is irritable because she can't sleep properly.

Tom: Maybe it's because she's been drinking so much espresso that she's irritable and can't sleep properly.

Tom hasn't shown that Dick's causal claim is false by raising the possibility of a common cause. But he does put Dick's claim in doubt. We have to check the other conditions for cause and effect to see which causal claim seems most likely.

Necessary Criteria for Cause and Effect
- The cause and effect happened (are true).
- It is (nearly) impossible for the cause to happen (be true) and the effect not to happen (be false), given the normal conditions.
- The cause precedes the effect.
- The cause makes a difference—if the cause had not happened, the effect would not have happened, given the normal conditions.
- There is no common cause.

Some *common errors* in reasoning about cause and effect:

Tracing the cause too far back in time   It's sometimes said that the cause must be close in space and time to the effect. But the astronomer is right when she says that a star shining caused the image on the photograph, even though that star is very far away, and the light took millions of years to arrive. The problem isn't how distant in time and space the cause is from the effect. The problem is how much has come between the cause and effect—whether we can specify the normal conditions.

   When we trace a cause too far back the problem is that the normal conditions begin to multiply.   There are too many conditions for us to imagine what would be necessary to establish that it is impossible for the cause to have been true and effect false. When you get that far, you know you've gone too far.

Reversing cause and effect   If reversing cause and effect sounds just as plausible as the original claim, then we should investigate the evidence further before making a judgment.

— Sitting too close to the TV ruins your eyesight.
— How do you know?
— Well, two of my high school friends used to sit really close to the TV, and both of them wear really thick glasses now.
— Maybe they sat so close because they had bad eyesight.

Looking too hard for a cause   We look for causes because we want to understand, so we can control our future. But sometimes the best we can say is that it's *coincidence*.

Before your jaw drops open in amazement when a friend tells you a piano fell on his teacher the day after your friend dreamt that he saw him in a recital, remember the law of large numbers: If it's possible, given long enough, it'll happen. After all, most of us dream—say one dream a night for fifty million adults in the U.S. That's three hundred and fifty million dreams per week. With the elasticity in interpreting dreams and what constitutes a "dream coming true," it would be amazing if a lot of dreams *didn't* "accurately predict the future."

But doesn't everything have a cause? Shouldn't we look for it? For much that happens in our lives we won't be able to figure out the cause—we just don't know enough. We must, normally, ascribe lots of happenings to chance, to coincidence, or else we have paranoia and end up paying a lot of money to phone psychics.

Post hoc ergo propter hoc ("after this, so because of this")
It's a bad argument that there is cause and effect just because one claim became true after another.

I scored well on that last exam and I was wearing my red striped shirt. I'd better wear it every time I take an exam.

The best prophylactic against making common mistakes in reasoning about causes is to *experiment.* Often we can't do an experiment, but we can do an imaginary experiment. That's what we've always done in checking for validity: *Imagine the possibilities.*

How to look for a cause
Conjecture possible causes, and then by experiment eliminate them until there is only one. Check that one: Does it make a difference? If the purported cause is eliminated, is there still the effect?

Examples

The cat made Spot run away.

Cause: What is the cause? It cannot be the cat, since things are not causes. Perhaps the cause is "A cat meowed close to Spot."

Effect: Spot ran away.

Cause and effect true: The effect is clearly true. The cause is highly plausible: Almost all things that meow are cats.

Cause precedes effect: Yes.

It is (nearly) impossible for the cause to be true and effect false: This is not clear. We have to establish the normal conditions. Spot normally chases cats, given the opportunity. But what is "given the opportunity"? We have no reason to believe he'll chase just any cat anywhere at any time at any distance from him. We do not know those normal conditions. At best we can say that it's highly unlikely in this situation that the cat could meow and Spot not chase it.

The cause makes a difference: Would Spot have run away even if the cat had not meowed near him? It would seem that under the normal conditions of a walk with Dick he wouldn't, since Dick is holding the leash loosely, not prepared for Spot to run away at any moment. But would Spot have chased the cat even if it had not meowed? Perhaps yes, if he had been aware of it.

So let's revise the cause to: "A cat meowed close to Spot, and he heard it." Now we can reasonably believe that the cause made a difference.

Is there a common cause? Perhaps the cat was hit by a meat truck and lots of meat fell out, and Spot ran away for that? No, Spot wouldn't have barked. Nor would he have growled.

Perhaps the cat is a hapless bystander in a fight between dogs, one of whom is Spot's friend. We do not know if this is the case. So it is possible that there is a common cause, but it seems very unlikely.

Evaluation: We have good reason to believe the original claim on the revised interpretation that the cause is "A cat meowed close to Spot, and he heard it."

These are the steps we should go through in establishing a causal claim. If we can show that one of them fails, though, then there's no need to check all the others.

Nancy caused the traffic accident.

Evaluation: We're interested in who or what was involved in the cause when we go about assigning blame or fault. But it's not just that Nancy exists. Rather, the cause is: Nancy didn't pay attention; the effect is: The cars collided. Is this really cause and effect? Did the cause make a difference? If Nancy had been paying attention would the cars still have collided? Since she was broadsided by a car running through a red light where a line of cars blocked her vision, it didn't matter that she was changing a CD at the time: The cars would have collided even if she had been paying attention, or so we all imagine. The purported cause didn't make a difference. It's not cause and effect.

Lack of rain caused the crops to fail.

Evaluation Cause: There was no rain. Effect: The crops failed. This example was true a few years ago in the Midwest. Causes need not be something active; almost any claim that describes the world could qualify as a cause.

Oxygen in the laboratory caused the match to burn.

Evaluation Harry works in a laboratory where there's supposed to be no oxygen. The materials are highly flammable, and he has to wear breathing gear. He was joking around with a friend and struck a match, thinking it wouldn't ignite. There was an explosion. It seems there was a leak in his face mask.

The normal conditions don't include "Oxygen is in the laboratory." That, along with Harry striking the match, caused the match to burn. *There may be several claims we want to say jointly are the cause*: Oxygen was in the laboratory; Harry carried matches into the laboratory with him; Harry struck the match. The rest can be relegated to the normal conditions.

Running over nails causes your tires to go flat.

Evaluation This is a plausible general causal claim. But it's wrong. There's not good inductive evidence. Lots of times we run over nails and our tires don't go flat. But sometimes they do. What's correct is: "Running over nails *can cause* your tires to go flat." That is, if the conditions are right, running over a nail will cause your tire to go flat.

The difference between *causes* and *can cause* is the difference between the normal conditions. For "causes" we feel we don't need much that isn't obvious; for "can cause" we feel that we could list claims, but they aren't perhaps "normal" ones we daily expect. This is discussed more in the Chapter 16.

God caused the universe.
Evaluation   This is not a causal claim. It's just a way of saying "God created the universe."

"When more and more people are thrown out of work, unemployment results." President Calvin Coolidge
Evaluation   This isn't cause and effect; it's a definition.

Birth causes death.
Evaluation   This is a general causal claim covering every particular claim like: "That this creature was born caused it to die." We have lots of inductive evidence: Socrates died. My dog died. President Kennedy died . . .
    The problem seems to be that though this is true, it's uninteresting. It's tracing the cause too far back. Being born should be part of the normal conditions when we have the effect that someone died.

Maria: Fear of getting fired causes me to get to work on time.
Evaluation   What is fear? Cause: Maria is afraid of getting fired. Effect: Maria gets to work on time.
    Is it possible for Maria to be afraid of getting fired and still not get to work on time? Certainly, but not, perhaps, under normal conditions: Maria sets her alarm; the electricity doesn't go off; there isn't bad weather; Maria doesn't oversleep; . . .
    But doesn't the causal claim mean it's because she's afraid that Maria makes sure that these claims will be true, or that she'll get to work even if one or more is false? She doesn't let herself oversleep due to her fear.
    In that case how can we judge whether what Maria said is true? It's easy to think of cases where the cause is true and effect false. So we have to add normal conditions. But that Maria gets to work regardless of conditions that aren't normal is what makes her

consider her fear to be the cause.

Subjective causes are often a matter of feeling, some sense
that we control what we do. They are often too vague for us to
classify as true or false.

Dick: Hold the steering wheel.
Zoe: What are you doing? Stop! Are you crazy?
Dick: I'm just taking my sweater off.
Zoe: I can't believe you did that. It's *so* dangerous.
Dick: Don't be silly. I've done it a thousand times before.
       Crash . . . Later
Dick: You had to turn the steering wheel!? That made us crash.

Evaluation The purported cause: Zoe turned the steering wheel.
The effect: The car crashed. The necessary criteria are satisfied.
But as they say in court, Zoe's turning the steering wheel is a
foreseeable consequence of Dick making her take the wheel,
which is the real cause. The normal conditions are not just what
has to be true before the cause, but also what will normally *follow*
the cause.

Dick: Wasn't that awful what happened to old Mr. Grzegorczyk?
Zoe: You mean those tree trimmers who dropped a huge branch
       on him and killed him?
Dick: You only got half the story. He'd had a heart attack in his
       car and pulled over to the side. He was lying on the pave-
       ment when the branch hit him and would have died anyway.

Evaluation What's the cause of death? Mr. Grzegorczyk would
have died anyway. So the tree branch falling on him wouldn't
have made a difference.

But the tree branch falling on him isn't a foreseeable consequence, part of the normal conditions of his stumbling out of his
car with a heart attack. It's an *intervening cause.*

The Treaty of Versailles caused World War II.

Evaluation The cause: The Treaty of Versailles was agreed to and
enforced. The effect: World War II occurred. To analyze a
conjecture like this an historian will write a book. The normal
conditions have to be spelled out. He has to show that it was a
foreseeable consequence of the enforcement of the Treaty of

Versailles that Germany would re-arm. But was it foreseeable that Chamberlain would back down over Czechoslovakia? More plausible is that the signing of the Treaty of Versailles is *a* cause, not *the* cause of World War II.

Poltergeists are making the pictures fall down from their hooks.
Evaluation To accept this, we have to believe that poltergeists exist. That's dubious. Worse, it's probably not *testable*: How could you determine if there are poltergeists? Dubious claims that aren't testable are the worst candidates for causes.

Tom: The only time I've had a really bad backache is right after I went bicycling early in the morning when it was so cold last week. Bicycling never bothered me before. So it must be the cold weather that caused my back to hurt after cycling.
Evaluation. Cause: It was cold when I went cycling. Effect: I got a backache. The criteria seem to be satisfied. But Tom may have overlooked another cause. He also had an upset stomach, so maybe it was the flu. Or maybe it was tension, since he'd had a fight with Suzy the night before. He'll have to try cycling in the cold again to find out. Even then he may be looking too hard for *the* cause, when it may be *a* cause. Another possibility: Tom will never know for sure.

My neighbor said it's been the worst season ever for allergies this spring, but I told her I hadn't had any bad days. Then today I started sneezing. Darn it—if only she hadn't told me.
Evaluation This may be cause and effect, but the evidence shouldn't convince. It's bad reasoning—*post hoc ergo propter hoc*.

A recent study showed that everyone who uses heroin started with marijuana. So smoking marijuana causes heroin use.
Evaluation And they all probably drank milk first, too. Without further evidence this is *post hoc ergo propter hoc*.

16 Cause in Populations

The difference between *causes* and *can cause* is what we see in analyzing cause in populations.

When we say, "Smoking causes lung cancer," what do we mean? If you smoke a cigarette you'll get cancer? If you smoke a lot of cigarettes this week, you'll get cancer? If you smoke 20 cigarettes a day for 40 years you'll get cancer? It can't be any of these, since we know smokers who did all that yet didn't get lung cancer, and the cause always has to follow the effect.

Cause in populations is usually explained as meaning that given the cause, there's a higher probability that the effect will be true than if there were not the cause. In this example, people who smoke have a much higher probability of getting lung cancer. But really we are talking about cause and effect just as we did before. Smoking lots of cigarettes over a long period of time will cause (inevitably) lung cancer. The problem is that we can't state, we have no idea how to state, nor is it likely that we'll ever be able to state, the normal conditions for smoking to cause cancer. Among other factors, there is diet, where one lives, exposure to pollution and other carcinogens, and one's genetic inheritance. But *if we knew exactly* we'd say: "Under the conditions _____ , smoking ___ number of cigarettes every day for ___ years will result in lung cancer."

Since we can't specify the normal conditions, the best

we can do is point to the evidence that convinces us that smoking is a cause of lung cancer and get an argument with a statistical conclusion: "People who continue to smoke two packs of cigarettes per day for ten years are ___% more likely (with margin of error of ___ %) to get lung cancer."

How do we establish cause in a population?

Controlled experiment: cause-to-effect This is our best evidence. We choose 10,000 people at random and ask 5,000 of them never to smoke and 5,000 of them to smoke a pack of cigarettes every day. We have two samples, one composed of those who are administered the cause, and one of those who are not, the latter called the ***control group***. We come back 20 years later to check how many in each group got lung cancer. If a lot more of the smokers got lung cancer, and the groups were representative of the population as a whole, and we can see no other *common thread* among those who got lung cancer, we'd be justified in saying that smoking causes lung cancer. (Of course such an experiment would be unethical, so we use animals instead, and then argue by analogy.)

Uncontrolled experiment: cause-to-effect Here we take two randomly chosen, representative samples of the general population for which we have factored out other possible causes of lung cancer, such as working in coal mines. One of the groups is composed of people who say they never smoke. One group is composed of people who say they smoke. We follow the groups and 15–20 years later check whether those who smoked got lung cancer more often. Since we think we've accounted for other common threads, smoking is the remaining common thread that may account for why the second group got cancer more often.

This is a *cause-to-effect* experiment, since we start with the suspected cause and see if the effect follows. But it is uncontrolled: Some people may stop smoking, some may begin, people may have quite variable diets—there may be a lot we'll have to factor out in trying to assess whether it's smoking that causes the extra cases of lung cancer.

Uncontrolled experiment: effect-to-cause   Here we look at as many people as possible who have lung cancer to see if there is some common thread that occurs in (almost all) their lives. We factor out those who worked in coal mines, we factor out those who lived in high pollution areas, those who drank a lot . . . . If it turns out that a much higher proportion of the remaining people smoked than in the general population, we have good evidence that smoking was the cause (the evaluation of this requires a knowledge of statistics). This is uncontrolled because how they got to the effect was unplanned, not within our control. And it is an *effect-to-cause* experiment because we start with the effect in the population and try to account for how it got there.

Examples

Reginald smoked two packs of cigarettes each day for thirty years. Reginald now has lung cancer. Reginald's smoking caused his lung cancer.

Evaluation   Is it possible for Reginald to have smoked two packs of cigarettes each day for thirty years and not get lung cancer? We can't state the normal conditions. So we invoke the statistical relation between smoking and lung cancer to say it is unlikely for the cause to be true and effect false.

Does the cause make a difference? Could Reginald have gotten lung cancer even if he had not smoked? Suppose we know that Reginald wasn't a coal miner, didn't work in a textile factory, and didn't live in a city with a very polluted atmosphere, all conditions that are associated with a higher probability of getting lung cancer. Then it is possible for Reginald to have gotten lung cancer anyway, since some people who have no other risks do get lung cancer. But it is very unlikely, since very few of those people do.

We have no reason to believe that there is a common cause. It may be that people with a certain biological make-up feel compelled to smoke, and that biological make-up also contributes to their getting lung cancer independently of their smoking. But we have no evidence of such a biological factor.

So assuming a few normal conditions, "Reginald's smoking caused his lung cancer" is as plausible as the strength of the statistical link between smoking and lung cancer, and the strength of the link between not smoking and not getting lung cancer. We must be careful, though, that we do not attribute the cause of the lung cancer to smoking just because we haven't thought of any other cause, especially if the statistical links aren't very strong.

Zoe: I can't understand Melinda. She's pregnant and she's drinking.

Dick: That's all baloney. I asked my mom, and she said she drank when she was pregnant with me. And I turned out fine.

Zoe: But think how much better you would have been if she hadn't.

Evaluation Zoe doesn't say but alludes to the cause in population claim that drinking during pregnancy causes birth defects or poor development of the child. That has been demonstrated: Many cause in population studies have been done that show there is a higher incidence of birth defects and developmental problems in children born to mothers who drink than to mothers who do not drink, and those defects and problems do not appear to arise from any other common factor.

Dick, however, makes a mistake: He confuses a cause in population claim with a general causal claim. He is right that his mother's experience would disprove the general causal claim, but it has no force against the cause in population claim.

Zoe's confusion is that she thinks there is a perfect correlation between drinking and physical or mental problems in the child, so that if Dick's mother had not drunk he would have been better, even if Zoe can't point to the particular way in which Dick would have been better. But the correlation isn't perfect, it's only a statistical link.

17 Explanations

> An explanation is an answer to a question
> that supposes some claim is true.

Why does the sun rise in the East? How does electricity
work? How come Spot gets a bath every week? Why didn't
you give me an A on the last exam?

We give explanations as answers to lots of different
kinds of questions: Why is this true? How do you do this?
What is your motive?

Our answers can be as varied as the questions. We can
give a story, a myth about why the world was created. We
can write a scientific treatise on how the muscles of the
esophagus work. We can give instructions for how to play a
guitar. We can draw a map.

But here we will focus on verbal explanations, particularly ones that answer the question "Why is this true?"

It's claims that are true or false. So in the kind of
explanations we'll look at we'll be trying to show why some
claim is true. That's different from an argument to show that
the claim is true. With an explanation we should already
have good reason to believe, say, "The sky is blue," and we
want to show what that claim follows from. The explanation
should provide us with other claims from which it follows.
Those claims won't be more plausible than the claim we're
trying to explain. That's a big difference from a good
argument, where the premises are supposed to be more
plausible than the conclusion. To remind us that explanations
and arguments are different, we use different terminology.

> ***Explanations*** An explanation is a collection of claims
> that can be understood as "E because of A, B, C, . . .".
> E is called the *explanandum*; and A, B, C, . . . are called
> the *explanans*.
>
> An ***inferential explanation*** is an explanation that
> can be understood as answering the question "Why is E
> (the explanandum) true?"

Sometimes the explanans by itself is called the explanation.

—Why is the sky blue?
—Because sunlight is refracted through the air in such a way that
    other wavelengths are diminished.
Inferential explanation. Explanandum: The sky is blue.
Explanans: Sunlight is refracted through the air in such a way that
wavelengths other than blue are diminished.

—Why does the blood circulate through the body?
—In order to bring oxygen and nutrients to every part of the body
    tissue.
Explanation, not inferential.

What must hold for an explanation to be good?

The explanandum is highly plausible We can't explain
what's dubious. In a good explanation, the explanandum
should be highly plausible.

Dick: Why is it that most people who call psychic hotlines are
        women?
Zoe: Wait a minute, what makes you think more women than
        men call psychic hotlines?

Dick has posed a *loaded question*: a request for an explanation of
a claim that is not highly plausible. Zoe has responded appro-
priately, asking for an argument to establish that "More women
than men call psychic hotlines" is true.

The explanans answers the right question Questions are
often ambiguous, and a good explanation to one reading of a

question can often be a bad explanation to another. If a
question is ambiguous, then that's a fault of the person asking
the question—we can't be expected to guess correctly what's
meant. An explanation is bad because it answers the wrong
question only when it's very clear what question is meant.

Mother: There were two pieces of cake in the cupboard. Why is
          there only one now?

Child: Because it was dark and I couldn't see the other piece.

Good explanation, but for the wrong question.

The explanans is plausible   In an inferential explanation
the claims doing the explaining are supposed to make clear
why the claim we are explaining is true. They can't do that if
they are implausible.

The sky is blue because there are blue globules in the atmosphere.
Bad explanation. "There are blue globules in the atmosphere" is
not plausible.

The explanation is not circular   We can't explain why a
claim is true by invoking the claim itself.

Zoe: Why can't you write today, Dick?

Dick: Because I have writer's block.

Bad explanation. "I have writer's block" just means that Dick can't wr

The explanation is valid or strong   In an inferential
explanation the truth of the explanandum is supposed to
follow from the truth of the explanans. So the relation
between the explanans and the explanandum should be valid
or strong, like the relation between the premises and
conclusion of a good argument.

Dogs lick their owners because they aren't cats.
Bad explanation. The relation of "Dogs lick their owners" to
"Dogs aren't cats" is neither valid nor strong, and there's no
obvious way to repair it.

As with arguments, *we allow that an explanation might
need repair.* An explanation "E because of A" might require
further claims to supplement the explanans.

A good explanation is not a good argument A good inferential explanation will have at least one premise that is less plausible than the explanandum.

Zoe: You drank three cocktails before dinner, a bottle of wine with dinner, then a couple of glasses of brandy. Anyone who drinks that much is going to get a headache.

Dick: I couldn't help it. Anything is better than listening to Tom talk about politics.

Good explanation, bad argument. Zoe offers a good explanation of why Dick has a headache:

> Anyone who drinks that much is going to have a headache.
> Therefore (explains why),
> Dick has a headache.

Judged as an argument this is bad, for it begs the question: It's a lot more obvious to Dick that he has a headache than that anyone who drinks that much is going to have a headache.

Minimal conditions for an inferential explanation to be good For an inferential explanation "E because of A, B, C, . . ." to be good all the following must hold:

1. E is highly plausible.
2. A, B, C, . . . answer the right question.
3. Each of A, B, C, . . . is plausible, but at least one of them is not more plausible than E.
4. The explanation is not "E because of D" where D is E itself or a simple rewriting of E.
5. "A, B, C, . . . therefore E" is valid or strong, possibly with respect to some plausible unstated claims.

Often we say that an explanation is *right* or *correct* rather than "good," and *wrong* rather than "bad."

Causal explanations Cause and effect reasoning can be evaluated as a kind of explanation, one that has to satisfy more than just the minimal conditions for a good inferential explanation. *If an explanation is given in terms of cause and effect, and it's good causal reasoning, and the explanation answers the right question, then the explanation is good; otherwise it is a bad explanation.*

Examples

Customer: Why did you call your coffee house *The Dog & Duck*?
Owner: Because *The Duck & Dog* doesn't sound good.
Bad explanation. The inference from explanans to explanandum is weak, and there is no obvious way to repair it.

Customer: Why did you call your coffee house *The Dog & Duck*?
Owner: Why not?
Bad explanation. Shifting the burden of proof is just as bad for explanations as for arguments.

Suzy: Why did Dick just get up and leave the room like that in the middle of what Tom was saying?
Zoe: Because he wanted to.
Bad explanation. It's obviously true that Dick wanted to leave the room, and, with further premises, that will give us the conclusion. But we want to know why Dick wanted to leave the room. Wanting to leave the room when Tom is talking is something unusual and requires further explanation.

An explanation is ***inadequate*** if the explanans leads to a further "Why?" Even if the explanans is obviously true, it may not be what we normally expect.

The gas has temperature 83° C because it has pressure 7 kg/cm^2 and volume 807 cm^3.
Good explanation, not causal. If the explanans and explanandum are true, this is good. But it's not causal, because the pressure, volume, and temperature all occur at the same time. Explanations that invoke a law that gives a correlation, such as this one that assumes Boyle's law, are inferential but not causal.

Zoe: I can see that this argument is bad. But why is it?
Dr. E: The argument is bad because it's weak, for example, Sheila could have been a rabbit or a herring.

Good explanation, not causal. An explanation in terms of rules or criteria isn't causal.

Dick woke up because Spot barked.
Good causal explanation. (See p. 77.)

Dr. E: I won't accept your homework late.
Maria: But I had a meeting I had to attend at work.
Dr. E: So? I don't count problems with employment as an adequate excuse for handing in late work.

Evaluation Maria has explained why she did not hand in the homework on time. She thinks she's also given an excuse, but Dr. E disagrees. What your employer will count as an excuse for being late may be unclear until you try a couple. What counts to a police officer as an excuse for speeding is very limited.
An explanation is not an excuse.

The relation of explanations to arguments

Dick, Zoe, and Spot are out for a walk in the countryside. Spot runs off and returns after five minutes. Dick notices that Spot has blood around his muzzle. And they both really notice that Spot stinks like a skunk. Dick turns to Zoe and says, "Spot must have killed a skunk. Look at the blood on his muzzle. And he smells like a skunk." Dick thinks:

> *Good Argument*
> Spot has blood on his muzzle. Spot smells like a skunk.
> Therefore, Spot killed a skunk.

He's left out some premises that he knows are as obvious to Zoe as to him:

> Spot isn't bleeding.
> Skunks aren't able to fight back very well.
> Normally when Spot draws a lot of blood from an
>   animal that is smaller than him, he kills it.
> Only skunks give off a characteristic odor that drenches
>   whoever or whatever is near if they are attacked.
> Dogs kill animals by biting them and typically drawing
>   blood.

Zoe replies, "Oh, that explains why he's got blood on his muzzle and smells so bad." That is, she takes the same claims and views them as an explanation, relative to the same unstated premises:

Good Explanation
Spot killed a skunk
Explains why Spot has blood on his muzzle and smells like a skunk.

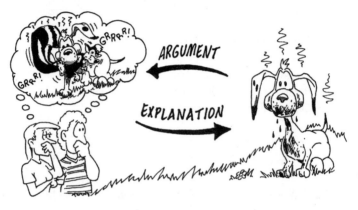

For Zoe's explanation to be good, "Spot killed a skunk" must be plausible. And it is, because of the argument that Dick gave. Sometimes an argument associated with an explanation is the best or only way to show that the explanans is true. We don't need to wait until Dick or Zoe finds the dead skunk.

> ***Explanations and associated arguments***
> For an inferential explanation
>   A explains E (assuming some claims P, Q, R, . . .),
> the *associated argument* to establish A is
>   E therefore A (assuming also P, Q, R, . . .).

For an explanation with many claims in the explanans, "A, B, C, . . . explain E," exchanging any one of A, B, C . . . with E yields an associated argument for that claim.

> ***Independent explanations*** An *independent*
> explanation is one where each claim in the explanans
> is either plausible or can be established by an
> associated argument. A *dependent* explanation is one
> where at least one claim in the explanans needs some
> evidence beyond the other claims in the explanans and
> explanandum to show that it is plausible.

Spot has blood on his muzzle and Spot smells like a skunk
because Spot killed a skunk.
Independent explanation

Spot chases cats because he sees cats as something good to eat and
because cats are smaller than him.
Dependent explanation."Cats are smaller than Spot" is plausible,
but "Spot sees cats as something good to eat" is not obviously true.
The associated argument for it is:

> Spot chases cats and cats are smaller than Spot.
> Therefore, Spot sees cats as something good to eat.

This is weak. Without more evidence for "Spot sees cats as
something good to eat" we shouldn't accept the explanation.

Explanations and predictions

Flo: Spot barks. And Wanda's dog Ralph barks. And
Dr. E's dogs Anubis and Juney bark. So all dogs bark.

Barb: Yeah. Let's go over to Maple Street and see if all the
dogs there bark, too.

Flo is generalizing. Relative to her experience it's a pretty
good generalization. Barb wants to test the generalization.

Suppose that A, B, C, D are given as inductive evidence
for a generalization G. (Some other plausible unstated
premises may also be needed, but we'll keep those in the
background.) Then we have that G explains A, B, C, D.

But if G is true, we can see that some other claims must

be true, instances of the generalization G, say L, M, N. If those are true, then G would explain them, too. For example, Rodolfo barks, Lady barks, Fido barks, . . .

That is, G *explains* A, B, C, D and *predicts* L, M, N, where *the difference between the explanation and the prediction is that in the explanation we know the explanandum is true, whereas we don't know if the prediction is true.*

Suppose we find that L, M, N are indeed true. Then the argument "A, B, C, D + L, M, N therefore G" is a better argument for G than we had before. At the very least it has more instances of the generalization as premises.

How do more instances of a generalization prove the generalization better? They can if (*i*) they are from different kinds of situations, that is A, B, C, D + L, M, N cover a more representative sample of possible instances of G than do just A, B, C, D. And this is typically what happens. We deduce claims from G for situations that we had not previously considered.

And (*ii*) because we had not previously considered the kind of instances L, M, N of the generalization G, we have some confidence that we haven't got G by manipulating the data, selecting situations that would establish just this hypothesis.

One of the best ways to test an hypothesis-generalization is to try to falsify it. Trying to falsify the generalization just means that we are consciously trying to come up with instances of the generalization to test that are as different as we can imagine from A, B, C, D. Trying to falsify is just a good way to ensure (*i*) and (*ii*). So we say an experiment *confirms* the explanans if it shows that a prediction is true.

> Consider the explanation offered by Torricelli for a fact that had intrigued his teacher Galileo; namely, that a lift pump drawing water from a well will not raise the water more than about 34 feet above the surface of a well. To account for this, Torricelli advanced the idea that the air above the water has weight and thus exerts pressure on the water in the well,

forcing it up the pump barrel when the piston is raised, for there is no air inside to balance the outside pressure. On this assumption the water can rise only to the point where its pressure on the surface of the well equals the pressure of the outside air on that surface, and the latter will therefore equal that of a water column about 34 feet high.

Torricelli offered an explanation, but the only evidence he had for the explanans, which was a generalization, was the explanandum.

> The explanatory force of this account hinges on the conception that the earth is surrounded by a "sea of air" that conforms to the basic laws governing the equilibrium of liquids in communicating vessels. And because Torricelli's explanation presupposed such general laws it yielded predictions concerning as yet unexamined phenomena. One of these was that if the water were replaced by mercury, whose specific gravity is about 14 times that of water, the air should counterbalance a column about 34/14 feet, or somewhat less than $2^1/_2$ feet, in length. This prediction was confirmed by Torricelli in the classic experiment that bears his name. In addition, the proposed explanation implies that at increasing altitudes above sea level, the length of the mercury column supported by air pressure should decrease because the weight of the counterbalancing air decreases. A careful test of this prediction was performed at the suggestion of Pascal only a few years after Torricelli had offered his explanation: Pascal's brother-in-law carried a mercury barometer (i.e., essentially a mercury column counterbalanced by the air pressure) to the top of the Puy-de-Dôme, measuring the length of the column at various elevations during the ascent and again during the descent; the readings were in splendid accord with the prediction.
>
> Carl G. Hempel, *Aspects of Scientific Explanation,* p. 365.

Predictions are made of further instances of the generalization or of consequences of the claim in the explanans; those are shown to be true; the explanans thus becomes more plausible because the associated argument for it is strengthened. The story is much the same for explanans that aren't generalizations, too.

Comparing explanations

Suppose we have two explanations of the same claim. Which is better? If one is right and the other wrong, the right one is better.

But suppose both are acceptable. Certainly we prefer the one that answers the right question and which doesn't leave us asking a further "Why?"

We also prefer a *simpler* explanation. By that we mean that its premises are more plausible, it is more clearly strong or valid (unstated premises are obvious and more plausible), and it has fewer steps.

There are subjective criteria that come into our evaluation of whether an explanation is good. Some work has been done on trying to make those criteria explicit, but the problem seems too difficult to be resolved soon. There may even be different criteria for different disciplines, for example biology vs. physics.

Some scientists think that if you have the best explanation, an explanans that could explain a lot, it must be true:

> It can hardly be supposed that a false theory would explain, in so satisfactory a manner as does the theory of natural selection, the several large classes of facts above specified [the geographical distribution of species, the existence of vestigial organs in animals, etc.]. It has recently been objected that this is an unsafe method of arguing; but it is a method used in judging of the common events of life, and has often been used by the greatest natural philosophers.
>
> Charles Darwin, *On the Origin of Species,* p. 476.

But if Darwin was right, why did scientists spend the next hundred years trying to confirm or disprove the hypothesis of natural selection? Only now do we believe that a somewhat revised version of Darwin's hypotheses are true. *Saying that a claim is true because it would explain a lot is arguing backwards*: From the premises (explanans) we can deduce true claims, so the premises are true. That kind of reasoning doesn't get any better by adding "This is the best explanation," since we don't have accepted criteria for what counts as the best explanation.

Fallacy of inference to the best explanation
Any argument like: "These claims give the best explanation, so they are true."

Scientists have high hopes for their hypotheses, and are motivated to investigate them if they appear to provide a better explanation than current theories. But the scientific community will soon correct a scientist if he thinks that just making an hypothesis establishes it as true. Torricelli had more sense than that.

> This the best explanation we have.
> = *This is a good hypothesis to investigate.*

Theories
A *theory* is a collection of claims that we either believe or wish to decide are true, and from which we can draw conclusions. For example, Newton's laws of motion constitute a theory.

Sometimes people will say that a theory explains something, for example, Newton's laws of motion explain the movement of the planets in the skies. But that's wrong. If someone were to ask you why the planets move in the sky, and you were to state Newton's laws of motion, you can be pretty sure the reaction would be "Huh?" A theory explains nothing. It is a deduction from a theory, an explanation using in the explanans some or all of the claims in the theory, that explains.

Besides, modern physics has replaced Newton's theories with Einstein's and quantum mechanics. So Newton's laws shouldn't explain anything, since they're false.

But can't we say that Newton's mechanics are correct relative to the quality of measurements involved, even though Newton's laws can't be derived from quantum mechanics? Or perhaps they can if a premise is added that we ignore certain small effects. But how is that part of the theory?

We can understand a lot of reasoning in science as reasoning by analogy: Making deductions or calculations from a theory is like reading a map correctly. Of course those deductions will be wrong if we are interested in more than the theory is meant to account for, just as we'd be wrong in saying there are no trees on a street because a street map didn't show them.

A scientific theory is a schematic representation of some part of the world. We draw conclusions from the representation (we calculate or deduce). The conclusion is said to apply to the world. The reasoning is legitimate so long as the differences between the representation and what is being represented don't matter. Newton's laws of motion allow us to make assertions about the world that are correct so long as we restrict what we pay attention to.

Laws in science are false when we expect them to represent all aspects of some particular part of our experience. What we have is any analogy: Newton's laws of motion are "just like" how moderately large inelastic objects interact at moderately low speeds; we can use those laws to make calculations so long as the differences don't matter.

One theory explains another that it contradicts if the new theory explains why the old theory worked as well as it did, and why it failed in the ways it failed. That is, we improve the map: By adding further assumptions, we can pay attention to more in our experience, and that accounts for the differences between the theories.

Teleological explanations
One day while cleaning out the small pond in my backyard I asked myself:

Why is there a filter on this wet-dry vacuum?

The wet-dry vacuum has a sponge-like filter, but the vacuum sucked up water a lot faster without it. I wondered if I could remove the filter.

I wanted to know the function of the filter. A causal explanation could be given starting with how someone once designed the vacuum with the filter, invoking what that person thought was the function of the filter. But most of that explanation would be beside the point. I didn't want to know why it is *true* that there's a filter on the vacuum, even though the truth of that claim is assumed in the question. I wanted to know what the *function* of the filter is. Some explanations should answer not "Why is this true?" but "What does this do?" or "Why would he or she do that?"

> ***Teleological explanations***   An explanation is *teleological* (tee-lee-ah-logical) if it invokes goals or functions, or uses claims in the explanans that can come true only after the explanandum is true.

Often a teleological explanation is offered when an inferential one should be used.

—Why is the missile going off in that direction?
—Because it wants to in order to hit that plane.

It's a bad *anthropomorphism* to ascribe goals to a missile: People, not missiles, have goals. We can and should replace this teleological explanation with an inferential explanation:

> The missile has been designed to go in the direction of the nearest source of heat comparable to the heat generated by a jet engine. The plane over there in that direction has a jet engine producing that kind of heat.

In science we prefer not to use teleological explanations, especially if we want to know why some claim is true. If the teleological explanation uses claims that can be true only after the explanandum is true, then it can't be causal (the cause has to precede the effect), and it would seem that the future is somehow affecting the past.

Further, a request for a teleological explanation assumes

the object has a function, or person or thing has a goal or motive. That is part of the claim that is assumed to be true and which requires an explanation. But often there is simply no motive, no function, no goal, or at least none we can discern. The right response, as to a loaded question, is to ask why the person thinks there is a function or motive.

The teleological fallacy Any argument that uses or requires as premise "This occurs in nature, therefore it has a purpose."

Dick (picking his nose): Why do humans get snot in their nose that dries up and has to be picked away? I can't understand what good it does.

Zoe: What makes you think there is a function? Can't some things just be? Maybe it just developed along with everything else.

The biggest problem with teleological explanations is that there is so little agreement about how to distinguish good ones from bad ones. In part that's because we don't have a very clear idea how to judge what counts as the function of something. At best, we have some minimal conditions for accepting a teleological explanation.

Minimal conditions for a teleological explanation to be good

1. The explanans is highly plausible.
2. The explanans answers the right question: not a question about what the explanandum follows from, but what the purpose or function or motive of some thing is.
3. The explanans does not ascribe motives or beliefs or goals to objects that cannot have those.

Examples

—Why will the Atlanta Braves win the pennant?
—Because they have the best pitching staff.

Evaluation This sounds like an explanation, but it isn't: "The Atlanta Braves will win the pennant" is not obviously true. It's a prediction. If the prediction comes true, then it will be further evidence for the general claim "The team with the best pitching staff always (usually?) wins the pennant."

Zoe: How was your walk?

Dick: Spot ran away again just a short way from the yard.

Zoe: We better get him. Why does he run away just before you come home?

Dick: It's just his age. He'll outgrow it. All dogs do.

Evaluation This sounded like a good explanation, until Dick and Zoe found that Spot chased a cat up a telephone pole in the field behind their house.

The explanation of the example is not bad. Perhaps in a year or two when Spot is better trained, he won't run away even to chase a cat. But there is a better explanation, one that is stronger: Spot ran away because he likes to chase cats.

Given a choice between explanations, the stronger one is the better explanation.

Me: Why do I have such pain in my back? It doesn't feel like a muscle cramp or a pinched nerve.

Doctor: A kidney stone would explain the pain. Kidney stones give that kind of pain, and it's in the right place for that.

Evaluation The doctor gave an explanation: Your back hurts because you have a kidney stone.

This would have been a good explanation if we'd had good reason to believe the explanans. But at that point the only reason we had was the associated argument, and that wasn't strong. Yet it was the best explanation we had.

So the doctor made predictions from the explanans:"A kidney stone would show up on an X-ray," "You would have an elevated white-blood cell count," "You would have blood in your urine." He tested each of these and found them false. He reasoned by reducing to the absurd that if the explanans were true, these would very likely be true; they are false; therefore, the explanans is very likely false. Hence the possible explanation turns out to be bad.

Nothing else was found, so by process of elimination the

doctor concluded that I had a severe sprain or strain, for which exercise and education were the only remedy.

Finding an explanation that is better than all others does not justify belief in the explanans. It only provides motive to investigate whether the proposed explanans is true.

—Why did Ponce de Leon wander all over the area we now
    call "Florida"?
—Because he was looking for the fountain of youth.

Evaluation   This is a teleological explanation. But it can be replaced with an inferential explanation: "Ponce de Leon wandered over Florida because he believed the fountain of youth was there."

Tom: Why is this piece of paper under the door?
Suzy: In order to keep the draft out.

Evaluation   Here is a teleological explanation in terms of the function of the object. But what if there is a draft under the door even with the paper there? We can talk about functions and unfulfilled functions, but it seems easier to answer the question by saying, "Because Suzy thought that putting the paper under the door would keep out the draft." That can be used as the explanans of an inferential explanation.

—Why do mammals have lungs?
—So that they can breathe.

Evaluation   This is not a good inferential explanation: "Mammals can breathe, therefore mammals have lungs" is either weak or circular. Yet this seems to be a good explanation if what is wanted is an answer about the function of lungs. In biology nowadays such explanations are usually replaced by ones in terms of evolutionary fitness.

Why does the blood circulate through the body?
(1) Because the heart pumps the blood through the arteries.
(2) To bring oxygen to every part of the body tissue.

Evaluation   The first explanation is a good causal one, if it answers the right question. The second is a good teleological one, if it answers the right question.

18 Fallacies

> We've seen lots of bad arguments. Each fits *at least* one of the conditions for not repairing an argument or else directly violates the Principle of Rational Discussion. Some kinds of these can be picked out and labeled as clearly unrepairable.

> **Fallacy**   A bad argument of one of the types that have been agreed to be so bad as to be unrepairable.

Here are the fallacies discussed in this text, along with a few others that are appeals to emotions. They are put into three categories.

Structural fallacies   Arguments that have one of the forms of a bad argument.

Affirming the consequent

If A then B   +   B
↓
A

Denying the antecedent

If A then B   +   not A
↓
not B

Arguing backwards with "all"

All A are B   +   x is B
↓
x is A

Arguing backwards with "almost all"

Almost all A are B   +   x is B
↓
x is A

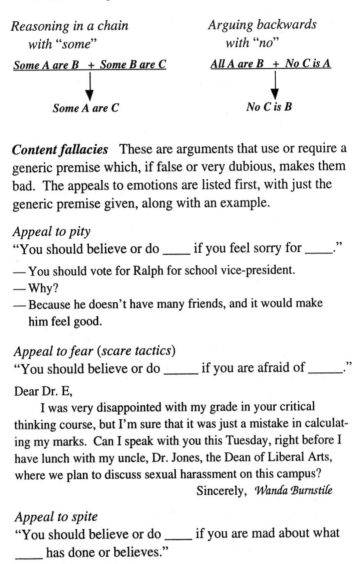

Reasoning in a chain
   with "some"

Some A are B + Some B are C

Some A are C

Arguing backwards
   with "no"

All A are B + No C is A

No C is B

Content fallacies   These are arguments that use or require a generic premise which, if false or very dubious, makes them bad. The appeals to emotions are listed first, with just the generic premise given, along with an example.

Appeal to pity
"You should believe or do _____ if you feel sorry for _____."

— You should vote for Ralph for school vice-president.
— Why?
— Because he doesn't have many friends, and it would make him feel good.

Appeal to fear (scare tactics)
"You should believe or do _____ if you are afraid of _____."

Dear Dr. E,
   I was very disappointed with my grade in your critical thinking course, but I'm sure that it was just a mistake in calculating my marks. Can I speak with you this Tuesday, right before I have lunch with my uncle, Dr. Jones, the Dean of Liberal Arts, where we plan to discuss sexual harassment on this campus?
                              Sincerely, *Wanda Burnstile*

Appeal to spite
"You should believe or do _____ if you are mad about what _____ has done or believes."

Dick: Hi, Tom. What's wrong with your car?
Tom: The battery's dead. Can you help me push it?
          Harry will steer.
Dick: Sure.
Zoe: (whispering) What are you doing, Dick? Don't you remember Tom wouldn't help you fix the fence last week?

Feel-good argument, apple polishing
"You should believe or do _____ if it makes you feel good."

I really deserve a passing grade in your course. I know that you're a fair grader, and you've always been terrific to everyone in the class. I admire how you handle the class, and I've enjoyed your teaching so much that it would be a pity if I didn't have something to show for it.

Wishful thinking is a feel-good argument you use on yourself.

Smoking can't cause cancer or I would have been dead a long time ago.

Calling in your debts
"You should believe or do _____ if you owe _____ a favor."

For an appeal to emotion, or for any of the other content fallacies listed below to be a bad argument the generic premise must be the only claim supporting the conclusion, where that isn't enough to justify the conclusion.

We should give to the American Friends Service Committee. They help people all over the world help themselves, and don't ask those they help whether they agree with them. They've been doing it well for nearly a century now. All those people who don't have running water or health care deserve our help. Poor little kids.

Evaluation This is an appeal to pity. But it is a legitimate one.

Appeal to authority
"(Almost) anything that _____ says about _____ is (probably) true."

Appeal to common belief
"If (almost) everyone else (in this group) believes it, then it's true."

Appeal to common practice
"If (almost) everyone else (in this group) does it, then it's O.K. to do."

Confusing objective and subjective
"This claim is subjective." / "This claim is objective."

Drawing the line
"If you can't make this difference precise, there is no difference."

False dilemma
Reasoning by excluding possibilities, but the "or" claim is false or very dubious.

Gambler's fallacy
"A run of this kind of events makes a run of contrary events more likely in order to even up the probabilities."

Inference to the best explanation
"These claims give the best explanation, so they are true."

Mistaking the person (group) for the claim
"(Almost) anything that _____ says about _____ is false."

Mistaking the person (group) for the argument
"(Almost) any argument that _____ gives about _____ is bad."

Phony refutation
"_____ has done or said _____, which shows that he or she does not believe the conclusion of his or her own argument" *and* "If someone does not believe the conclusion of his or her own argument, the argument is bad."

Post hoc ergo propter hoc
"This happened after that, so it's cause and effect."

Slippery slope
(Reasoning in a chain with conditionals where one of them is false or enough of them are dubious so that the conclusion doesn't follow.)

The teleological fallacy
"This occurs in nature, therefore it has a purpose."

Violations of the rules of rational discussion   Some of
these aren't fallacies, because they aren't arguments. They're
collected here for ready reference of bad ways to convince.

Begging the question
The point of an argument is to convince that a claim is true.
So if the premises of an argument are no more plausible than
the conclusion, it's a bad argument.

Relevance
Sometimes people say a premise or premises aren't relevant
to the conclusion. But that's not a category of fallacy, just an
observation that the argument is so weak you can't imagine
any way to repair it.

Ridicule
Making someone or something the butt of a joke in order to
convince.

Strawman
It's easier to knock down someone's argument if you
misrepresent it, putting words in the other person's mouth.

Shifting the burden of proof
It's easier to ask for a disproof of your claim than to prove it
yourself.

Slanters
Concealing claims that are dubious by misleading use of
language.

These labels for bad arguments are like names that go on
pigeonholes: This bad argument can go in here, that argument
there, this one fits into perhaps two or three of the pigeonholes, this argument, no, it doesn't fit into any, so we'll have
to evaluate it from scratch. If you forget the labels, you can
still remember the style of analysis, how to look for what's
going wrong. That's what's important. The labels are just

shorthand for doing the hard work of explaining what's bad in an argument.

You've learned a lot of labels and can manage to make yourself unbearable to your friends by pointing out the bad arguments they make. That's not the point.

We want to learn, to exchange ideas, not stifle disagreements. We want to convince and educate, and to that end we must learn to judge bad arguments.

Some arguments are so bad there's no point in trying to repair them. Start over.

Some arguments are bad because the other person intends to mislead you. In that case the Principle of Rational Discussion is violated. There's no point continuing the discussion. These labels and analyses are then prophylactics against being taken in.

But often enough the person making the bad argument isn't aware that he or she has changed the subject or brought in emotions where they don't belong. Be gentle. Point out the problem. Educate. Maturity isn't pointing a finger at someone and laughing. Ask the other person to fill in the argument, to add more claims. Then you can, perhaps, learn something, and the other person can, too.

19 Evaluating Reasoning

> We summarize the methods for evaluating the various kinds of reasoning studied here.

Arguments

1. Read the entire passage and decide if there's an argument. If so, identify the conclusion and number every sentence or clause that might be a claim.

2. For each numbered part, decide if it is a claim:
   a. Is it too vague or ambiguous?
   b. If it's vague, could we clear that up by looking at the rest of the argument? Are the words implicitly defined?
   c. If it's too vague, scratch it out as noise.
   d. If it uses slanters, reword it neutrally.

3. Identify the claims that lead directly to the conclusion.

4. Identify any subarguments that are meant to support the claims that lead directly to the conclusion.

5. See if the obvious objections have been considered.
   a. List ones that occur to you as you read the passage.
   b. See if they have been answered.

6. Note which claims in the argument are unsupported, and evaluate whether they are plausible.

7. Evaluate each subargument as either valid/invalid or on the strong–weak scale.
   a. Note if the argument is one of the fallacies or valid types we've discussed.
   b. If it is not valid or strong, can it be repaired?
   c. If it can be repaired, do so and evaluate any added premises.

8. Evaluate the entire argument as either valid/invalid or on the strong–weak scale.
   Repeat (a)–(c) of (7) for the entire argument.

9. Decide whether the argument is good.

That's a lot to do. But not all the steps are needed each time. If you spot that you have an argument that is one of the bad types we've discussed, you can dismiss it. If key words are too vague to consider the conclusion or crucial parts as claims, you can dismiss the reasoning. But often you'll have to go through all these steps. Or you could just go with your gut reaction—throwing out all the work you've done in learning to reason well. Remember: It is irrational to accept that an argument is good, yet still reject the conclusion. If you think there's something wrong with an argument, find it.

Analogies
1. Is this an argument? What is the conclusion?

2. What is the comparison?

3. What are the premises (the sides of the comparison)?

4. What are the similarities?

5. Can we state the similarities as premises and find a general principle that covers the two sides?

6. Does the general principle really apply to both sides? What about the differences?

7. Evaluate the passage using the steps for arguments.

Generalizing

1. Is this an argument?
2. Identify the sample and the population.
3. Are the three premises for a generalization plausible?
   a. The sample is representative.
   b. The sample is big enough.
   c. The sample is studied well.
4. Evaluate the passage using the steps for arguments.

Cause and Effect Reasoning

1. Can you identify the purported cause and effect as claims? Are they too vague? Are they true?
2. Decide if the purported cause precedes the effect.
3. Evaluate whether it is (nearly) impossible for the claim describing the cause to be true and the claim describing the effect to be false, relative to some normal conditions.
4. Decide whether the cause makes a difference: If there were no cause, would the effect still have happened?
5. Make sure that none of the obvious mistakes are made:
   a. It's not cause and effect reversed.
   b. It's not *post hoc ergo propter hoc.*
   c. It's not tracing the cause too far back.
6. Decide whether you can conclude there's cause and effect.

Cause in Populations

1. Identify the kind of experiment that is used to support the conclusion: controlled or uncontrolled; cause to effect, or effect to cause.
2. Decide whether you should accept the results of the experiment.
   a. Was it conducted well? (Use the methods for evaluating generalizations.)
   b. Does it really support the conclusion? (Use the steps for evaluating arguments and cause and effect.)
3. Decide whether the argument is good.

Inferential Explanations
1. Is this an explanation of why some claim is true?
2. Identify the explanandum, what's being explained, and the explanans, the claims doing the explaining.
3. Is the explanandum true?
4. Does the explanation answer the right question?
5. Is the explanation circular?
6. Is the explanation causal? If so, use the methods for evaluating causal reasoning.
7. Decide whether each of the claims in the explanans is plausible.
    a. Is one of those less plausible than the explanans?
    b. If one is not plausible, decide whether one of the associated arguments will establish it.
8. Is the explanans testable?
    Will further experiments confirm the explanans?
9. Determine whether the explanation is valid or strong, possibly with respect to some unstated claims.
10. Is there a simpler explanation?
11. Decide whether the explanation is good.

Teleological Explanations
1. Is this an explanation of the function or goal of something?
2. Could an inferential explanation be substituted?
3. Is the explanation attributing motives or goals to something that cannot have them?
4. Does the explanation answer the right question?
5. Identify the explanandum, what's being explained, and the explanans, the claims doing the explaining.
6. Decide whether each of the claims in the explanans is plausible.
7. Decide whether the explanation is good.

20 Writing Good Arguments

- If you can't spell, if you can't write complete sentences, if you leave words out, then you can't convince anyone. All the reader's effort will be spent trying to decipher what you intended to say.

- If you don't have an argument, literary style won't salvage your essay.

- If the issue is vague, use definitions or rewrite the issue completely to make a precise claim to deliberate.

- Don't make a clear issue vague by appealing to some common but meaningless phrase, such as "This is a free country."

- Beware of questions used as claims. The reader might not answer them the way you do.

- Your premises must be highly plausible, and there must be glue, something that connects the premises to the conclusion. Your argument must be impervious to the questions: So? Why?

- Don't claim more than you actually prove.

- There is a trade-off: You can make your argument strong, but perhaps only at the expense of a rather dubious premise. Or you can make all your premises clearly true, but leave out the dubious premise that is needed to make the argument

strong. Given the choice, opt for making the argument
strong. If it's weak, no one should accept the conclusion.
And if it's weak because of an unstated premise, it is better
to have that premise stated explicitly so it can be the object
of debate.

- Your reader should be able to follow how your argument is
put together. Indicator words are essential.

- Your argument won't get any better by weaseling with
"I believe that" or "I feel that." Your reader probably
won't care about your feelings, and they won't establish the
truth of your conclusion.

- Your argument should be able to withstand the obvious
counterarguments. It's wise to consider them in your essay.

- For some issues, the best argument may be one which
concludes that we should suspend judgment.

- Slanters turn off those you might want to convince.
Fallacies just convince the careful reader that you're
dumb or devious.

   You should be able to distinguish a good argument from
a bad one. Use the critical abilities you've developed to read
your own work. Learn to stand outside your work and judge
it, as you would judge an argument made by someone else.

21 Making Decisions

The skills you've learned here can help you make better decisions.

Making a decision is making a choice. You have options. Make a list for and against the claim—all the pros and cons you can think of. Make the best argument for each side. Then your decision should be easy: Choose the option for which there is the best argument. Making decisions is no more than being very careful in constructing arguments for your choices.

But there may be more than two choices. Your first step should be to list all the options and give an argument that these really are the only options, and not a false dilemma.

Suppose you do all that, and you still feel there's something wrong. You see that the best argument is for the option you feel isn't right. You have a gut reaction that it's the wrong decision. Then you're missing something. Don't be irrational. You know when confronted with an argument that appears good yet whose conclusion seems false, you must show that the argument is weak or a premise is implausible. Go back to your pro and con lists.

Now that your reasoning has been sharpened, you can understand more, you can avoid being duped. And, we hope, you will reason well with those you love and work with and need to convince. And you can make better decisions. But whether you will do so depends not just on method, not just on the tools of reasoning, but on your goals, your ends. And that depends on virtue.

Index